Other Lives, Bends in the Road, and What-Ifs

BOOKS BY RICK SCHMIDT

FICTION

Two Girls In High Rafters

The Greatest Second-Chance Frog Queen

Secrets of Men and Women

Cold, The 1918-19 Siberian Escape of Captain Ewald Loeffler

Blackmale

Kennedy's Twins

Black President--The Story of JFK's Secret Sons

NON-FICTION

THE FILMS OF RICK SCHMIDT 1975-2015

SLEEPER TRILOGY—Three Undiscovered First Features 1973-1983.

A TREASURY OF ART, (PART 1, 2, 3)— Undiscovered Works From the Collection of Artist/Photographer Julie Schachter and Filmmaker Rick Schmidt , 1966-2022.

THE ART OF JULIE SCHACHTER— 50 Years of Sculptures, Paintings, and Drawings, 1972-2022

THE ART OF JULIA EASTBERG: An Important Undiscovered Woman Artist, from Oakland/Richmond, California, Hawaii, and Port Townsend, Washington

NEW DARK AGES —How a Punk Movie EMERALD CITIES Got Its IMPROV

Twelve Dead Frogs and Other Stories, a Filmmaker's Memoir

The Miracle of Morgan's Cake, Production Secrets of a $15,000 IMPROV Sundance Feature

Extreme DV

Feature Filmmaking at Used-Car Prices

How to Make Money With Your Video Camera

Other Lives, Bends in the Road, and What-Ifs

A Novel by Rick Schmidt

Front Cover: Rick Schmidt, Mills College, Oakland,
California, 2015. Photo by Pat Kelley.

Back Cover: Rick Schmidt poses for MFA graduation,
CCA, 1971—w/"natural" wig, cast bronze film case,
fireman's coat, and East Oakland studio phone #.
Photo by Robert Arnold.

1st EDITION
COPYRIGHT © 2023

AUTHOR'S NOTE

For Julie

An Introduction

Where to begin? All those *plum* opportunities to have lived another life. All those many times that I could have just allowed myself to flow in some other direction. You'll find that my end-game of life could have been completely different had I just blinked and made different choices.

I use the word *blinked* because that's what happened to a friend who said he did just that—had a one-night fling which caused his wife to move out/the marriage ending. He had an affair with a student. I asked what happened, and he said, "Rick, I blinked." In other words, he made a choice based on certain emotional impulses and it had cost him his happy home.

Many of the stories up ahead are about that kind of blinking, where a certain opportunity would have taken my life into a right or left turn from what I thought I should continue with. Here's a partial list of chapters to come—various Alternate Universes, not my real life. (1) I could have ended up living in an Oregon commune, free log cabin I'd build with help, free organic food from the garden—a *stress-free* life, so it seemed—if I'd just taken up their offer during my hitchhike trip in July, 1969 (the first *what-if* story, coming up).

Or, (2), I could have taken an offer to become a "grill man" at a popular Hyannis Port/Cape Cod restaurant (Bobby Kennedy ate there with his family before my dishwashing gig, late summer of 1964). Of course, I would have been vulnerable to being drafted and sent to Vietnam a few years after that!

(3) A complicated series of events *would not* have gotten me a wife and kids, if I hadn't removed a six-pack of beer from the refrigerator at a shared college apartment. My roommate, a "friend" from Boston, threw me out (you'll learn it was about more than just beer), and I inadvertently met my future wife, by renting her cottage on my way to campus that next morning to avoid homelessness.

To continue with the "What Ifs," this next one (4,) made sure I didn't become a businessman (my entrepreneurial future crushed). I might have been happily making a profit selling things if my parents hadn't scolded me, age 11, when I tried to sell my amusement-park-won very large stuffed panda to my 9-year-old sister.

And (5) to slightly backtrack, if I hadn't continued my (a) road trip out of Pensacola to Boston because (b) I'd *blinked* after winning the affection of a gorgeous young woman who I met at a rock concert at the Pensacola beach pavilion and taken her back to my motel room *for a beer*—she was a rare beauty, probably under-age—I might have spent a decade or more in a jail cell/chain gang for a statuary rape charge (average incarceration; 10-15 years), then later also missed out on (c) a dishwashing job in Hyannis Port (June, 1964), followed by (d) not borrowed beer (two months later), which, in turn, would have erased all the steps to my real life as I know it, including getting married, having kids, going to art school, becoming a filmmaker, writing a "used-car" filmmaking book (which helped launch Hollywood careers of Kevin Smith and Vin Diesel), and so on. Yes, *everything would have been changed,* by just a couple well-placed blinks. You get the picture.

Maybe this modest book will help someone,

somewhere, make a crucial <u>better choice</u>, instead of just heading down the path of least resistance. Hope so!

In any case, Please enjoy my Alternate Universes.

TABLE OF CONTENTS

CHAPTER ONE
Living at Life Magazine's
Secret Oregon Commune

Ahead is my first fable about a bend in the road, about the commune life in Oregon I originally turned down in 1969 and where that decision could have led, had my spirit been so moved in that direction. Around Grant's Pass, OR, with my thumb out, I got picked up by a long-haired hippie in a VW bug, and was driven through the woods off the highway, to a large-scale commune that—unbeknownst to me—had just been immortalized by a Life magazine photographer. I had previously hooked up with a self-described "millionaire" guy I had met while we hitched together along a lonely stretch of road, and he was there as well. When I was given a choice of joining the commune that choice would have rocked my world.

In this first chapter I examine this other life I might have led. Each person gets offered certain choices that could have caused a cosmic shift in their lives. Here's my *real-life* account of when I was offered a free place to live—free food, free housing in a self-built log cabin, new friends (maybe even a new girlfriend)—adding up to a supposedly carefree, "hippie-style" living situation.

*   *   *

Real Commune Story

At a summer break from the third year in art college I decided I needed a vacation, some time off from all the work I'd been involved with—creating cast metal art works, grinding away the rough edges (usually filing surfaces, sometimes going to fine polishing) to get the exact look and presence the metal concepts demanded. At any rate, I thought it was time for a change of scenery from my small, one-room apartment near the art school (my rent in 1969 dollars was $20/month). My life, in that period of time, had revolved around working in the school foundry, and walking or driving a few blocks home at night, so it was time to break out of that routine. It was early in my separation from my first wife and kids, which had occurred at the beginning of that summer, and now it was Fall. But I missed my kids and had made occasional visits to see them in Berkeley—of course thoughts of them really never left my mind as I tried to rebuild a single life again, alone.

Regarding a vacation trip somewhere—there wasn't really money for that. The foundry usage and the metal I poured was free. My tuition was covered by the full scholarship and I even got paid for helping undergraduate/graduate students, as their TA. But no airline ticket for me to Seattle (my rough destination), or somewhere out of Oakland, CA, was in the cards.

The solution to a trip to the Pacific Northwest was to hitchhike there. After all, I'd successfully hitched to RISD (Rhode Island School of Design) in 1968, magically arriving there in just three days, spending two at the art school, meeting people, seeing art, and then returning in just three more—an eight-day round trip. If you're interested, read the rash of stories generated from that crazy trip in my memoir, <u>Twelve Dead Frogs and Other Stories</u>).

OK. so no big deal to hitchhike up there. How

bad could it be? Just up the West Coast. Mainly, aside from the structure of a destination penciled into my brain, what I appreciated from using hitchhiking as a means to travel was that it offered several actual advantages to performing a trip in the standard manner. Not needing reservations in hotels/motels meant I would never get stressed about being either too early or late for any arrival. And because of the way in which hitching demands you live in the present (waiting beside the road for a ride...) there were no loose ends about trip schedules that generally creates stress one can't control . Like maintaining a vehicle—oil and gas, tire pressure, parking, unloading suitcases, worrying about valuables/security in the motel rooms, where to eat meals (what does the AAA book recommend?). All that disappeared when you hitchhike.

So, aside from the obvious concern about getting rides from strangers, or waiting too long for a ride, there was really no obstacle to having a completely happy, responsibility-free travel experience. So off I went.

And it worked pretty well right from the start. I got several long rides heading north, and soon found myself rolling past the California state line into Oregon. Yes, the hitching concept was paying off. And even the "Illegal to Hitchhike" signs along the Highway 101 didn't seem to threaten my flow. I chose to just ignore that negative sign-painting. Obviously, some authority figures/political entities/institutions in Oregon had voted to halt travelers like me (anti-hippie legislation, etc.), but I felt I'd be fine, just rolling through that state without looking back. Nothing was going to dampen my refreshing journey and nothing did—never even saw a highway Patrolman.

Around the area of Grant's Pass I was dropped off by my current good-Samaritan driver, and even that occurrence was a pleasurable one. With feet on the ground, I was suddenly transported to storybook farmlands—lush greens everywhere, inhaling a new freshness of country air, all the newness that I had hoped would come my way on my vacation. The concept of getting "a change of scenery" was certainly working well.

After an hour or more of not getting a ride I decided to stroll up ahead along the highway, and soon afterward, rounding a bend, I came across another fellow hitcher. I gave a wave to him and got one back. I decided to maintain a reasonable distance (100' perhaps) so as not to crowd his space, but after a while he called out to me, "Maybe we should hitchhike together?" I returned, "OK!" and strolled up to join him.

As I approached his location he became more of a distinct person than just an outline of a human figure in the distance. I took in his friendly vibe and noticed his attributes. He was a bit older than me (I was 26 then), thinking maybe ahead by ten years. He was a handsome guy in what I'd call "the classic way," with a full and mature manly face, evenly sun-tanned, but what stood out more during this initial cursory overview was that, despite his casual clothes and jacket, he resembled a young executive type, someone who might have emerged from some glassed-in cubical at a bank or somewhere. He could have been a person who would confer with you over the granting of a car loan, or a real estate purchase. In other words, he seemed a bit out of place for partnering up with a scruffy art student on some lonely stretch of highway, in the middle of nowhere.

His hair was close cropped, but extremely well-coiffured—another sign that he was out of place as a hitchhiker. Some professional barber knew what he/she was doing. And although he was wearing jeans and a warm, patterned wool shirt, I could easily sense that his everyday attire was actually a well-pressed suit jacket, tie and trousers that held a sharp crease.

His face gave it all away too—clean shaven, paired with a confidence that comes from having and making money, holding an important job of some sort. His intelligence twinkled in his eyes. This was a real adult, the kind I usually try to avoid. Still, he was so affable he quickly disarmed any possible hesitation on my part. I was happy to meet someone new, enjoying the possibility of being energized by that temporary companionship. (If you read my memoir, you'll know from chapter headings listed in the Table of Contents that I'm apt to experience unusual things while hanging in the limbo of hitching along the road. Some of those chapter headings include; Flagstaff Flatfoot, Temptress, Burning, Dead Meat, Dog Bite (not of me), to name a few.)

Anyway, we certainly had time to talk since no

ride was immediately forthcoming. And what he talked about was highly fascinating. He said he'd been a millionaire a couple times over. What that meant, he added, was that he had made lots of money—and lost money—initially in a real estate deal for a tract housing development outside of Phoenix. But it had gone bust. He didn't seem too sad about that, though, as he described with confidence brimming, how he knew he could raise another pile of cash from another source. So I was right in assuming that he was some kind of executive.

But not in every instance. He went on to describe being just another working stiff, in a factory, back to doing that kind of grunt work for another half-year, after his financial loss. How then, I wondered, could that ever deliver the additional millions that he spoke about re-earning? What he said next was eye-opening.

He had worked at a bottling plant—can't remember if it was Coca Cola or Ginger Ale—and said that while there he had made some important observations, identifying how the plant could save a lot of money. He said it had taken him about six months to figure that out. He'd then called a meeting with the top brass, and made them an offer, he emphasized, that they could hardly refuse. (My interest was certainly peaked at this point).

He announced to the executives in the head office that he'd discovered a way for them to save a million dollars a year, and that they could either pay him $50,000 for that information, or... cut him a check for everything they saved over a million. He explained (just before our ride rolled up) that they took the $50K every time.

As his story swirled around in my head, we were magically transported farther down the highway in a rather crowded VW bug, him in the small back seat, me riding shotgun. Our driver, an obvious hippie—long hair, work clothes—was genial and ready to do his spiel. Mixing his words with the occasional "Praise the Lord," he asked if we were hungry. Of course, he got two Yes's back. He then added, "Then I'll drive you to my home, where there's good food, good women, and love, Praise the Lord."

Suddenly he veered off the highway, onto a

narrow dirt road that I hadn't seen coming, cloaked as it was in a loose spread of bushes just feet from the asphault. In less that a minute we rolled up to a fairly large settlement of log cabins, plus a much larger structure in the distance (*Our community lodge*, he explained). It was also impossible to miss the large and productive garden in the open field, along with several hippie-looking women (attractive, I could see), and their male hippie counterparts, hoeing away and gathering items in baskets. It was a fully-inhabited Oregon commune.

Just as I emerged from his VW he pointed to a half-built log cabin with a stout-looking hippie guy sawing a log on a sawhorse and asked me if I'd like that, like to build a little house like that one, to live in, live there, no rent, free. I can't remember my immediate answer, stunned as I was by the question. But I was flattered by the possibility, of course.

Next, our guide walked us over to several long tables covered with an array of vegetables, fresh from the garden, he said. Another commune member explained that Life magazine had just been there, taking pictures, of that very meal, along with "teepees and people, garden and lodge."

"You're eating the same food from their pictures," he added, before inviting us—my millionaire and me—to fill our plates.

And the food was delicious. While munching on the free food our driver/guide couldn't help giving us a few more doses of salesmanship, listing the different plants they raised; almonds for almond butter, lettuce, parsley, turnips, celery, radishes, walnut. But I was suddenly very tired. I can barely remember sitting against a tree and just being happy to be so thoroughly fed. That's the point where I either passed out from lack of sleep, or from one of the ingredients in the free meal.

Bam, I woke up with a start. My face was half-against the ground, in the dirt. Too stunned to start moving yet, I watched a little girl out of my partially opened eye. She was dressed in a tattered and somewhat dirty "white" dress, holding a piece of broken mirror in her hands, while admiring herself. How long had I been out? I was thankful it was still light out, but what day? How long had I been sleeping? Rip Van Winkle-time? Hopefully not 20 years.

I rose slowly, disoriented, and tried to get my bearings. I spotted the workers in the field a distance away, saw some other children playing on the ground nearby. Didn't see my millionaire right then, but he appeared shortly thereafter—he'd been given a royal tour of some buildings, including the main lodge.

"So," began our benefactor, "do you think you'd like to stay here?" Some pretty women too...for you. Praise the Lord."

"Maybe," I answered, adding, "Don't think so, though."

Although still drowsy from my maybe-marijuana-infused meal, still partially stoned, I was still able to recall that I had a life in Oakland, art to make, kids from my 1st marriage to visit, even bills to pay, and wasn't quite prepared to make that kind of snap decision, to instantly give all that up!

As soon as the driver realized that we were lost causes we were quickly driven back to the highway, dumped back to our future destiny of awaiting rides along a highway. But what if I had said, yes?

Here comes my ALTERNATE Universe Story

#1, me running my fantasy about the life I would have had, by mumbling the simple word, *OK*. For that scenario to happen, it would have just taken an off-the-cuff affirmative answer.

If I had thought that maybe a new life could help me avoid some of those past pitfalls, the extra pressures of my normal life, I might have decided to take the commune route as offered. Here's what may have happened if I'd just blinked. So, *YES*, I'm imagining the result of just voicing the few words, *COUNT ME IN!*

And *Yes,* I want to saw logs and build a tiny home there in the middle of the Oregon woods. *Yes*, I want good, fresh vegetables, eating free meals that are sometimes laced with marijuana (what had knocked me out so powerfully?). *Yes*, maybe I can "mate" with one of the several young and spry unattached women you pointed out in the garden. *Yes* to it all, and goodbye to attending art college, to paying rent, to babysitting my kids from a failed first marriage.

ALTERNATE UNIVERSE #1

On that first afternoon of my new life, as the VW
driver drove my millionaire-hitching buddy back off of
the commune's property, back toward the highway, I
waved my goodbye. I watched as they pulled away,
past the Life Magazine's food display, back into the
high foliage that camouflaged the road in and out. I
had certainly appreciated the stranger's money tip,
learning how to earn an easy $50K (or more) if I ever
landed in a factory job again and could make some
money-savings observations like he did. Yeah, I now
had some unusual financial future—of sorts. But that
was neither here nor there, since I was now a resident
of a wooded settlement in the middle of the Grant's
Pass forest preserve.

I followed Bate ("Bait" is how I initially
thought his name was spelled when he first spoke it) to
the lodge after he returned, and started meeting my new
compatriots. I'll put them in handy categories, starting
with the men-folk, and will do my best to list and
describe each one whom I came in contact with, with
my women-list following shortly thereafter.

THE MEN (and actually there were some boys among them, if you consider the point of separation being around age 13)

The #1 man I met was called "Francis" (I tried not to laugh when he said his last name—"Pickering"), had sandy-ish red hair, some pimples on his face/cheeks and forehead, was about six feet tall (we were close to eye-to-eye—I'm 5' 11 3/4"), pretty skinny (his legs inside his jeans seemed to leave a lot of space between his flesh and the clothing that surrounded them) and somewhere around my age of 25-6. He was fostering a mustache without much luck (pretty skimpy facial hair, if you ask me), but was nicely self-deprecating about it. "Call me Semi, for semi-bearded," he said, laughingly. He was a friendly guy who I could relate to pretty well. He said he was an art school dropout and I confessed the same. So, simpatico!

#2 man I met was named "Charlie," just like a teacher I had had earlier in sculpture class. Charlie didn't really press anyone to do anything, just brought it up lightly in conversation, with his simple questions.

"Do you think we have enough gardeners?" he

would ask, and there seemed to be only one correct answer. Since my initial contact there at the commune with Bait (I'll keep spelling his name this way, until later in the story when I got corrected!) had said that no one did any work <u>unless their spirit moved them</u> to do it, so I was interested in how that axiom really worked in real-life, day-to-day existence. Did the garden always get all the planting in, all the shoveling, enough watering and the harvest done on time? It was hard to believe that something that important—the bread-basket of the whole endeavor—was really left up to human whims. Maybe Charlie was the gentle reminder, the soft-spoken manager of that kind of operation. I was sure I'd learn what was true, and not so much, in the days ahead.

For my first night as a new member of the communal club I began to worry about missing some of my basic items I didn't have on hand there, like: (1) a warm sleeping bag, (2) decent boots (I had just worn my everyday sneakers to hitch), (3) changes of underwear (I had only a couple in my backpack), and a few other incidentals. At least I did have a toothbrush, though I was at the end of my toothpaste tube. So, those small, stupid-seeming worries came creeping in. Fortunately my mind didn't click into the really BIG concerns until the following day.

The Women (mainly the first female commune member who swept me off my feet).

As night descended, I followed Charlie's advice and just kind of secured a part of the lodge closest to the fireplace—fire was built and lit by a pretty girl/woman named (I thought) "Marmalade." Her actual name was Mary Lade, which would finally be spoken clearly after we spent an unexpected night of lovemaking. Yes, that very first night I got lucky! Here's how it happened.

She, of course, was well aware of me watching her build the fire, while I laid there on a fairly thin rug—my bed— reclined there with my coat scrunched up as a pillow, trying to be as comfortable as possible. I sort of pretended everything was OK when it really wasn't. I was used to at least a normal mattress, like back at my normal apartment. She looked up at me a few times, smiled broadly, and I smiled back. No words were spoken, but like any red-blooded man in his mid-twenties I checked her out. Bent over as she was, I couldn't help getting a little turned on to her slim body, pretty face, long brown hair. She was a highly desirable member of the opposite sex. And maybe I looked good to her too, having some youth and newness-to-the-commune in my favor..

As soon as she finished with the fire—I immediately felt warmer just seeing the flames lifting up off the wood—she removed her firewood-handling gloves, placed them neatly on a counter to the right, eased herself over to me, lifted my chin with her delicate hand and planted a big kiss on my lips. Wow, that was unexpected, but all so beautiful.

We fell into the long kiss and the touching—caressing—followed, right there on the rug and hard wood floor. When she rose to a kneeling position and offered me her hand I gave mine, then stood up and followed, accompanying her toward a closed door, which she opened to reveal her cozy little bedroom and cubby hole with hanging dresses, work boots below, a tiny table with a candle and ashtray on top. I was brought down onto the bed with the smallest of prompting as we kissed some more. She then broke away and scooped up a pre-rolled joint from the tray, struck a match, lit up, took a good drag and passed it my way. If only to be polite (I wasn't much of a smoker of weed) I took my puff, held in the smoke—quite long actually—and almost immediately felt the buzz. I handed it back and she took another.

Now I was floating. It could certainly have been attributed to hitchhiking exhaustion, like what made me pass out after the meal, but whatever my physiological state was leading in to this pleasant interaction, I was 100% stoned, 100% turned on, and she made pretty good use of that, I'd say.

Pure sex, with a complete stranger who hadn't said hardly a single word, was how my initiation to communal life began. I certainly had no complaints! I hadn't been with a woman for awhile and that made it all the more intense and fulfilling. Of course, I passed out right after finishing, and woke up in a very relaxed and happy mood. When I heard the sound of some quiet singing, from my new girlfriend, Marmalade, that was just a heavenly bonus. Maybe joining the commune on a whim, making an instant decision with no regard to all the ramifications that awaited me, had been a smart decision after all. Great, even. Hell yes it was! I hadn't felt that good in a long, long time. Being temporarily unencumbered by all the junk that modern daily life presented was a terrific relief (or so I thought, in that temporarily delusional state...). I'd been ushered into the warm nest of a lovely young woman, after being fed by Bait's delicious offering of the Life Magazine meal. And I would soon build my own free cabin housing (no rent!). Everything finally made sense.

Good food, free housing, and free healthy food. And a powerful dose of free love. What on earth could be missing from that spectacular combination? Maybe you, dear reader, can venture a guess. I'm sure you have, by now, identified how I could hit my first snag with all this "perfect life" seduction. It actually took me a day or two (two more intense love-making nights) to somehow come to my senses about what kinds of messes I'd left behind. Somehow, my pleasure-addled brain had broken clear enough to realize that I had some very unpleasant chores to do in this regard.

It would be no fun to call my ex-wife and explain where I was, and how I couldn't continue my usual babysitting weekends with my two dear children from the breakup. And secondly, what would my landlord think, when I announced I was gone halfway through the month, having left all my crap inside, personal belongings still cluttering the place.

While I'd now planned to inadvertently supply a customary "two-week notice" (how considerate of me) I'd have to figure out if I had any friend good enough to drag all my shit out of the space before the two weeks elapsed, maybe even do some cleaning—sweeping, perhaps mopping the bathroom floor not to mention scrubbing the toilet bowl. Does anyone have a friend like that? I kinda doubted it. So, who did I have? I'd had to ponder that question a bit longer, while trying to use my considerable powers of denial as the first communal days passed by.

The second day (maybe it was the third—too much weed and lovemaking made it hard to exactly know) I had been brought out to the garden by my lover, who hand-guided me through the particular plants she knew needed tending. With her guidance I was soon watering properly, getting a quick lesson in pruning too, then gathering up debris and dumping waste into a mulch box. Nothing like some good physical activity to help one forget about ordering new bank checks (where was the nearest bank?), and paying odd bills which I could barely remember (phone, electricity).   Could a phone call to someone, somewhere, help to start cleaning up my normal existence? Oh, oh!

I set upon my chores with a greater ferocity than I could have imagined. Please FORGET, you stupid brain! Luckily, the sun felt good, made me sweat. And the warm-but-also-cool summer weather continued through the two hours I was out there. It was just my past responsibilities that started to rain on my parade.

"Hello," I called into the pay phone as my ex-wife grumbled about accepting the reverse charges.

"What's going on, Rick?"

Ugh, where to begin, I wondered. "I'm, not at home, so sorry I had to call collect..." I began.

She cut off my words, quickly demanding answers., "I get that, but what's this all about."

"Umm, I'm in Oregon right now, and I don't think…"

That's as far as I got, before she erupted.

"Why there? And what about tonight, picking up kids?"

Shit. I had lost track of the days. I'd been thinking that Friday was tomorrow. Shit, SHIT!

"I'm real sorry, but can't get back for the pickup..."

"When can you?"

Now the real shit was going to hit the fan. "Well, I can't at all this weekend. Sorry." (I waited for the obvious bad reaction, the anger and accusations, whatever was brewing in her "hate-box" that day, for her Ex—ME.

"Damn. That's really fucked. I have things I was going to do.

"I'm really pissed!"

All I had left was meekly adding, "Sorry again." I remember my guts feeling sick at about this point. When I heard the click of her hanging up I knew that there would be an even more horrible Part-2 call in my future, the one where she'd hate me more than ever when I announced they'd be no more babysitting by me, because I'm living in Oregon now.

So began the daily dance between my life in Eden, the ongoing Adam & Eve existence and the deadly moments of trying to make amends, manage retribution phone calls, fielding misunderstood moments with friends, contacting fellow artist friends who psychically depended on me continuing to work besides them (hard to admit that that was over). And finally, dealing with my mother a half-state away would be no fun at all; She would be furious that I was defaulting on both my career and my parenting responsibilities, letting her down with no good explanation   All that, all those messes were the trade-off for my so-called "Stress-Free Living In The Woods."

As the mostly-warm days of summer extended through June—Grant's Pass continuing the traditional warming trends—I set upon constructing my living quarters. I had to wait a couple days to get my hands on the axe I'd spotted on that first day hitching in. So, at first, I just hung around inside the lodge, and began to interact more with my commune's other men and women. And that was easy, because once they associated me with Marmalade, they treated me quite like family. Finally, with the axe firmly in my hands, I began to select trees and chop them down. And actually none of that process, from cutting down mostly same-size trees, to clearing off the branches and dragging the timbre back to my building site, was very difficult. I used my still-youthful energy to get logs notched properly, and the walls quickly became erected. Of course with Marma as my rooting section, even helpmate on her days away from the garden, it did actually progress smoothly, to a point where a little house began to appear somewhat magically.

She kept hinting that "our home" would be, *Oh so cozy*. And while she somewhat soft-peddled it, I did hear her say something about, *Even for three*. And we all know what that meant, don't we?

More kids! At least one more, from a woman whose son or daughter would happily call her mommy Marmalade. Her off-side comment got me right back to thinking about the life I had left behind. What was going to happen to my relationship with my current children? Especially after the next phone call to my ex-wife, where I'd have to admit that I was, in fact, not going to be available for any future babysitting, because I now...was expecting! Holly shit, would she get mad with those words. I'd be attacked with a barrage of questions, and no way to duck any of them.

"What the fuck are you still doing in Oregon?" My first answer would just make her madder. I decided to try and give it a patina of logic by incorporating Marma into my answer: "Well, I've joined my new girlfriend here...to live in a new commune..ity."

That bought me maybe six more seconds of phone silence, which calmed me down maybe 20%, though I knew another broadside was coming.

"I thought you were going to graduate school—making sculptures—right? To get a teaching job or something after."

She didn't really give me time to respond.

"So you're just dropping that whole thing, your scholarship, the TA income, the whole normal thing...for gardening?"

Now I was supposed to speak again, say something she wanted to hear. My mind raced, but detected no satisfactory answers.

"Well?" she said, impatient as hell.

I figured I had to say something. Anything. Of

course, I couldn't help digging a deeper hole.

"Don't I have the right to have a life. A mate, without half of my existence still being dragged along by my marriage to you? That ended six years ago..."

She said nothing...yet. Stupidly, I continued.

"It felt like I needed a new start, and this is it."

Silence still.

"Of course I'll miss the kids."

Now I got the wrath of that trigger sentence.

"What kids? They won't even know or remember you in six months."

I stuttered here.

"But they...do know I love them, have pictures, some presents I gave..."

And here was where the vengeance of a divorced wife reared it's full ugly head.

"They won't know you because I'll make sure they don't."

"That's fuckin' evil," I said, and could feel my blood rushing in my veins. "You wouldn't really...?"

Her voice seemed completely calm as she said her final piece.

"You won't help with babysitting, or send any

support money that the court ordered. Our deal was that you babysit instead of giving money, but that's off now. Talk to me again when you've come to your senses. I think...you're a major fuckup."

And click.

Being hung up on like that didn't help my mood any. Only Marma did, with her devoted lovemaking that evening. But upon rising—Marm already out in the garden—it dawned on me that, unbelievably, my EX might have point. My main thought, at that 7AM moment was, what if I actually get Marm pregnant (Heaven forbid!)? Then I'd be in a crossfire of TWO potentially angry women, each of whom expected me to deliver chunks of my time, my life, to the childrearing. Then there'd be TWO families I'd be letting down. That's the moment when I started to formulate my extraction from the commune, before winter set in, before I impregnated my girlfriend (that is...if I hadn't done so already!).

That's when it hit me that I needed to flee. That shoe, if it did fall in 6 weeks or so, would happen long after I got back to Oakland and grad school. Yes, I actually found myself ready to settle on just ONE totally screwed up life. And no little, half-built 100 square foot log cabin residence would keep me in those woods, with the wool over my eyes.

I was only two weeks into my "forever commune-living" when I activated my escape plan. How far was it from the lodge and garden to the highway? Maybe a mile-and-a-half? I could walk it, run if necessary, then stick out my thumb, facing south. When I realized the full extent of what I was forsaking by that Oregon fantasy I suddenly panicked, then went through all the emotions of feeling like a total asshole.

No art-making, no free metal for casting, no income from TA work. And I'd signed up for a video class and that would also be gone, whatever that was. Maybe it could have led to moviemaking. Who knows.

And bye bye bank account with any money in it—I'd given Bait a check for him to cash in Portland, for my new boots, and coat for winter. I'd let that $100 fuckin' go, and figured I'd be happy if half was still left in the account (of course it wouldn't be!) It would have been emptied, money all gone, then closed.

I would also lose my 1939 Dodge pickup. Parked on the street when I left—what was it...two weeks ago? Three?—it would have been towed by now…or maybe not yet. There was still time. Maybe. How fuckin' insane had I been, just jumping into the commune without any real thinking or planning?

Gone.

I got myself gone—quickly snuck through the foilage to the highway and hitched the rides, got myself back to Oakland unbelievably fast, ran some of the way, barely arrived back before I'd lost everything. Hello again to a college degree in art, some income, free art supplies, even a reserved seat in the future video class (filmmaking!), and finally art friends who forgave almost anything. More importantly than I could fully understand, I somehow still retained the tiniest respect from an ex-wife for what she called, *seeing the light*, and from my sweet kids—by retaining my cheap apartment I could still care for them on weekends. And I still had my truck (amazingly, it hadn't been towed!). Hell…I'd gotten back <u>my mind!</u>

****

****

Ok, OK, OK! I didn't really decide to join the

Oregon commune. And please don't think that the people at the commune were bad or even questionable. The commune there in Oregon was a well-run, well-managed operation, peopled with mostly college grads, even including an MD on the premises. You can read about it and check out the Life Magazine pictures I've included.

Maybe you can imagine what it felt like, cracking open the Life magazine issue on "The Youth Communes" and laying eyes on the very meal that had sent me into that afternoon "Rip Van" slumber. Not every day a person sees evidence like that—photographs from a dream they almost embraced (see LIFE cover and meal, p. 160-62).

Of course, the offer to join the commune didn't really fit in my life's flow at that time. Things in my life were working pretty well. I did have freedom to do art, and even got paid to be there during my years during foundry classes and studio time beyond scheduled periods. With an ample amount of free time, and the good fortune of having the company of my young kids on weekends, plus a fun and dependable old 1939 Dodge pickup truck I bought for just $25 (it went for ten years without the need for a tune-up), I don't think that my rational brain would ever have allowed for this "commune fantasy" to have ever occurred. But stranger things have happened to people in a weak moment!

CHAPTER TWO
Winning my "Profit Panda" in Chicago's
Riverview Amusement Park (1953)

I'll now take you back, way back into my earliest
childhood, where other choices and avenues were
awaiting, possibly even in position to derail the future
life that I ultimately experienced.

Here's some first imprinting that may have
rattled and disrupted the person I became, at around 11
years old, when I tried to make a profit on a huge
stuffed panda that I won at an amusement park in the
far reaches of the South Side of Chicago, state of
Illinois.

This next section is important, not for any
decision I did or didn't make, but for a certain attitude
that was impressed on me by my parents. I think it
clearly describes their aversion to me making a profit
on an object I bought/won at an amusement park, and
that bleeds over into my not ever trying to become an
American capitalist in my future. Anyway, you'll see
what happened up ahead, when I threw two perfect
hardball pitches in a row.

Real Panda Story

As a young kid I had visited the Marshall Fields and Company department store in downtown Chicago several times—I bought my first baseball mitt there; a leather Raleigh, right-hander, shortstop edition, saving up for many months to collect the twelve dollars it cost. This incident, about the panda, had to have occurred just a couple years earlier, when I was 10-11, in any case way before my family moved to the West Coast in 1956.

Anyway, while in the department store at some point I had noticed a very large panda I wanted, which cost all of $25. With inflation rates up to present day, 2023, the present cost would be close to $270. So that stuffed toy was an extremely expensive item for a young child like me to contemplate, let alone acquire.

The next time I laid eyes on that large-sized panda was at the Riverview Amusement Park, way past Chicago's downtown "Loop" area. I can't remember who took me there, maybe on a school trip or a friend's birthday outing, but in any case I was impressed to see it again, and watched as adults paid 50 cents for two hardballs they'd throw—the panda could be won by just knocking two fur-covered "cats" off a shelf. That glimpse of the game at that concession stand imprinted the idea of acquiring it firmly in my brain.   In the privacy of my room on the South Side of Chicago, in my parent's house on Kimbark Avenue, just about a mile from the 47th Street Illinois Central (IC) train station, I began to form a plan to win the huge toy.

I decided to try and travel back there, figuring that if I brought much of my savings—up to $10 or so—I could try my luck at winning. Somehow, I believed that I could throw those two balls accurately enough, knock the furry sticks off the rail after a few tries. I wasn't exactly caught up in an over-confident mood, more like an obsession and wishful thinking. But I didn't really take the odds of failing into account.

Beyond my knowledge, the figures I had to topple were so well-designed that the game booth rarely lost one to the "marks" who tried to impress their girlfriends with their ball-throwing. The trick of an arcade—not losing any panda prizes—was that the fur stick-figure cats on the rails that the players saw were neatly covered with a disarming furry outer surface. You had to throw two perfect balls, to precisely strike the very narrow rod inside the fuzzy cats. Customers saw maybe ten pairs of cats available to target, and stood a good fifteen feet or more feet back from the targets. And the base of each cat was enclosed somewhat tightly in the high ridge that ran along the rail. If the ball made contact too low on the rod you might jiggle the cat a bit, but it wouldn't fall. "The sweet spot" was only a tiny portion of what appeared to be an easy target. Like hitting a one-inch by one-half--inch spot, with two balls, twice in a row, from a good distance away. Hard throws from a variety of older kids and adults would rarely deliver a prize-winning moment. That's the game I decided to play.

As a dyslexic kid—I wasn't identified as such back then (in 1953)—I had a somewhat unique approach to spending my days alone. All my mother knew was that I "went out to play," and returned before dark. No one was aware that I occasionally went all the way to downtown Chicago, eight miles away by the IC (if I had a coin for traveling each direction), to see a movie.

I would travel there by myself, first walking the four blocks from my house to 47th, then right about five or six blocks more to the train station, pay my 25 cents for the eight-mile ride to the Loop, and spend another 50-cents to see a movie. Sometimes, I even treated myself to a hamburger and coke (and additional $1.25) in a cafe near the State or Chicago theatres I'll call them "movie palaces" because they were HUGE, especially to a young kid like me. The balconies where I liked to sit were incredibly vast.

At any rate, I already had those kinds of completely unmonitored excursions under my belt. Call them secret if you like, because since I didn't involve any friends I could just travel anywhere I wanted, if I got back before 5PM. And it never occurred to me that I was doing something special or wrong. It had none of that kind of charge for me. I just knew how to enjoy movies, and how to travel to see them.

So when the day arrived, the one when I decided to go and try to win my panda, I stuffed all my allowance and Christmas money––around $10 in half dollars––into my pockets, along with some quarters for the train, and walked my usual route to the IC. I always enjoyed riding in the lead car, with the wind washing across my face through the wide-open front, only a thick chain across the opening there as security (cigar smokers usually filled the small space, standing all around behind me).

Arriving in the Loop, I went to a nearby bus stop and asked the driver how to get to Riverview Park. He told me to get aboard, and handed me a transfer slip, saying he'd let me know when to get off, when to transfer to a second bus. The full bus journey was something like riding the first 100 blocks, then taking bus #2 another two hundred more, to finally arrive at the park.

Once at the familiar entrance to Riverview, I retraced the steps I'd learned from the birthday party, and was soon standing right in front of the "panda" arcade booth. Two big pandas hung prominently on the wall to entice people to try their luck. Two balls for 50-cents.

After watching several adults try and fail to win anything I plunked down my first half-dollar. There was no initial success, but throw after throw I adjusted my aim, as the half-dollars disappeared. Five more tries went by (ten throws) as I slowly understood what it took to knock those cats off their shelves. I became aware that hitting too low didn't work, so I threw higher. When I finally hit a cat in the head it tumbled off. Now I just had to do that twice in a row.

I may be wrong about how much I spent that day, but I had decided to go for broke in any case. When I got an occasional cat to fall I could hear people somewhere behind me clapping or cheering. But I didn't look back. *The little kid keeps throwing balls*, I believe I heard someone exclaim.

With each new throw, and analyzing the results, I improved my results. I honed in on my targets and honed my accuracy, and finally came up with the two perfect strikes, both cats toppling off their perches. Maybe the crowd reacted, but I don't remember hearing anything. I just have a clear picture of the booth guy handing me the immense stuffed animal—just about half of my size—and me having trouble getting my arms in a good grip before heading back to the bus.

I can now only imagine what people thought, as they watched a little kid struggle along with that gigantic toy. Almost Candid Camera-worthy. At any rate, the buses and a train got me back to the South Side, and all I had to do was traverse a short distance to my house.

Finally I got it inside and set it down on my bed, and my sister immediately gushed over it. She could barely contain herself, because she had also wanted it ferociously when we were in Marshal Fields. I guess I let her hold it, cuddle it, and she was in heaven. Finally, I broke down and decided to sell it to her.

I had spent maybe as much as $7 to win it, between $7-10 anyway, because I remember that I had 16 half-dollar coins in my collection, and needed some cash for bus and train. So what should I charge for it?

Since the department store cost was $25, I figured that $12 was fair. She would get it for half price and I would get all my savings back plus a few extra dollars to re-buy half-dollar coins for my collection.   She agreed whole-heartedly, paid me with her dollar bills, picked it up and scurried off to enjoy it in her own bedroom.

I guess I missed it, but not as much as she seemed to need it, and I needed money to buy a delicious-smelling new leather baseball glove I had tried on at the same store. I planned to go there and get it soon. But within the next hour or two my parents—mainly my father I think—got wind of the panda deal, and they got all bent out of shape.

"How dare you try to make money off your sister?"

"That's not what a good brother does."

"It would be nice if you just gave her the panda."

"Don't you want to be a nice brother?"

"You need to give her money back."

I was hit squarely with all that flack, all the kind of family pressure they could muster. I was not then capable of verbally explaining my side, how I had spent all my money on it, how I had traveled the many miles to get it (secretly, they would have said). So I gave my sister the free panda, and had to begin saving up allowances all over again, certain that I would never again try to make a profit off anything, from anyone, in the future.

Their castigating had pretty well cured me of desiring the "life of sales." No used-car salesman's job for me. I would go on to make movies at "used-car prices" instead.

*   *   *

BUT...what if I'd been *praised* (instead of chastised), complimented as having made a <u>good</u>, solid business-like transaction?   Different parents, like those of my later California classmates—many of them lived in special gated communities on private coastline, wealthy businessmen, lawyers and the like—may have overtly celebrated my business acumen, given me confidence that I had a future in creating equitable situations where both parties gain in equal ways, from an exchange of goods and services.

<u>REAL STORY—A Business-First "Friend"</u>

I remember having one particular "California friendship" during high school where my buddy explained all the fun we'd have together, "hanging around" his father's Christmas Tree lot. Oh boy! What fun! We could help people select trees, hammer on stands, and take their money. So, I joined him for several prime tree-selling days, helping out (for free). I was too happy to be around someone who acted like they liked me, to notice I was being used.

Later, it became painfully clear what was going on. He called me up to say that a very special trip was taking place, to Death Valley, organized by his father, the camp counselor, who had that business of leading such excursions for kids—10-days of high adventure! I pressed my parents to sign me up, they paid the fee, and when I arrived at the parking lot early one Christmas vacation morning to depart, my "friend" was nowhere in sight. When I realized that I was stuck as the oldest kid amongst a bunch of much younger kids I begged my parents to cancel, but they said it was too late, and off I rolled. My friend's father did say that he'd make me "his assistant" to help with the younger members of the caravan.

I did enjoy Death Valley—Scotty's Castle, Furnace Creek Ranch, all of—but certainly had nothing more to do with the con-artist kid the lawyer-father had raised. A sad example of the kind of profit-driven life that manipulates and feeds off others.

At another point, when I was in my early twenties, I enrolled in a class that trained real estate salesmen, in Hayward, California, a half-hour drive from my Berkeley home. There was a written test presented on the first day I attended, in which the question was asked, *What would you do if you earned over your monthly nut with a sale?* I wrote, "I'd work twice as hard to double that!" figuring that was the answer they would desire. So, Right Answer: *Greed is good.* But I never went back to the next session. I understood that my need to seek approval would be dangerously dragging me into a life of compromised values, to say the least.

Well, my California friend with his father's Christmas tree lot and tours of Death Valley was certainly an entrepreneur-in-training. There seems to be an inherent quality of "taking advantage of others for profit" built into the basic money-making spirit. For millions of citizens, this is the "American way of life" (and certainly in other countries as well). You've got your CEOs, business executives, managers, and down the corporate ladder the simple 'bosses,' whose jobs are telling/ordering workers to do the heavy-lifting at a much-reduced salary. Somewhere in this discussion comes the concept of "slavery," but let's put that off for a few pages. Mainly, this book section is about what would have happened to me if I'd gone whole-hog for a life based on making a profit, become an entrepreneur, often at the expense of others.

(Wikipedia Definition: Entrepreneurship is the act of being an entrepreneur, or the owner or manager of a business enterprise who, by risk and initiative, attempts to make profits).

REAL STORY—"Most Marbles" Flashback.

One day, when I was picking up my original film footage at W.A. Palmer Lab in San Francisco, around 1975, the lab manager felt like giving me a lesson in business. Here's what he said:

"Rick, you don't seem to understand. Life is a game of marbles, and whoever has the most at the end wins."

That's what the dog-eat-dog business world is like. And if you have to throw someone under the bus to get all those marbles...it's basically understood (at least by your business cronies). So I say, *Thanks parents*, for a life where money-earning/profit-chasing doesn't rule my every waking moment!

CHAPTER THREE
A Gorgeous (& Dangerous) Florida Girl

This next segment is imagining what would have happened to my life if it had taken a completely different direction. It leads from improving my college grades (parents awarded me with $500 for raising my college grades to a B+, which I used for a trip to Pensacola, Florida, where I met a gorgeous under-aged girl at a dance (she picked me, to give her phone# to) to what could have become *my horribly risky "date,"* if the laws of statutory rape in Florida had needed to be applied!

On that same trip I won a dishwashing job in Cape Cod, Hyannis, MA, being hired over the 100+ kids my age who were vying for summer jobs. That gig was an actual miracle of timing, as you will learn.

So I'll impart why these events could have easily derailed my "normal" life. But first, this story must begin with my attending meetings with a psychologist my mother signed me up with, to help me get better grades, which in turn got me the funding for the trip East.

REAL STORY—Summer Shrink

After my mother became aware of my poor college grades, she resorted to signing me up with a psychologist whose job it was to analyze the potential of a client and—in my case, measure my so-called untapped aptitude with regard to my achieving better grades in mostly-engineering classes.

Subjects ahead in that career path included Differential Equations, Statics and Dynamics (plotting orbits, etc.), Strength of Materials (I was set to take that class in the following year, Chemistry 1 & 2, and others. So suddenly, in the mist of my summer break, after sophomore year, I found myself attending these early morning meetings; not exactly the fun and relaxed summer I had envisioned. But I went along with my mother's wishes. She said he would report his finding to her and me after the five or six sessions.

He mainly ran tests on my English, math, reading comprehension, and then quizzed me verbally while I sat there in my chair. I do remember one question he asked; "Do you ever lie?" I said, *No*, at which point he called me a liar. He said, "Everybody lies." OK. Umm. All I can say is, I was making it a point in my life of not lying, not deluding myself, and I guess I was a little surprised at his response.

One other morning, at the 9AM slot, he brought out a little block of wood from a box and set it in front of me. There were two thin nails hammered into the topside, about three inches apart. He explained that this was a dexterity test. He then added two containers to the desk, one filled with metal washers with holes in the centers, the other containing little lengths of thin metal tubing, hollow in the middle. He explained I needed to stack as many of the washer-tube-washers on each nail post as quickly as I could. It was a test of dexterity, he said. And, GO! After I exerted myself and heard the buzzer he counted up the results and said, disparagingly, that I had done horribly, gotten one of the worst scores he'd ever seen. Oh. I asked if I could try again, maybe the next morning? I didn't bother to make an excuse, didn't tell him that I'd gotten to bed around 5AM that morning and was barely awake for the test. Anyway, I requested to take the strange test again, and he agreed.

The next morning I repeated the task—washers-tubes-washers, over and over, as fast as I could. And guess what he said? I had gotten the highest score he'd ever seen. So much for testing accuracy.

His final report to my mother stated that I should be getting grades of B+ or higher in engineering, and the next semester I worked hard to realize that, for my mother's sake if not my own. I didn't fool around—hard not to when you attend something called "the playboy college" (U. of Arizona's rep at the time), but I kept to the straight and narrow. I just attended classes and directly returned to my little apartment, maintaining my boring study routine for several months. Ultimately, the grades were good, and my father rewarded me with cash as I've said, which I quickly converted into Traveler's Checks.

I took off that summer of '64 roughly half a day after the bank visit, driving my '58 Plymouth sedan East, taking the southern route; Arizona, Texas, Georgia, toward Pensacola to visit a friend there. When I say I didn't consult any roadmaps please

understand that it's not as difficult as it sounds. Just
follow the signs that say "East" instead of "West" or
"North."

REAL STORY—Pensacola Trip/The Girl

My "Police Special" Plymouth sedan ran off two 4-
barrel carburetors, along with an "hydraulic Isky" cam
I had personally installed with a mechanic friend's
help. That gave it some especially fast acceleration
between 30 and 50 mph. That used car my father had
gifted me with had been retired from local police work
in Santa Barbara, California, much faster than the
normal production models of 1958.

Another improvement I'd made had been
getting "tuck and roll" brown leather upholstery in
Tijuana, Mexico for $120, when a high school friend,
Alan, and I had traveled there. So the engine was hot-
rodded, the inside pretty fancy (I'd also moved the gear
shift from the steering column down to the floor), and
all this would figure into my story coming next, about
winning the girl in Pensacola, which could have caused
my life to have disastorous legal problems.

So in June, 1964, with a fat bankroll, I happily

left Santa Barbara, a California coastal town, headed down coastal Highway 101, hitting LA a hundred miles later, then intersecting with Highway 15, zipping past Victorville, Barstow, a route I knew well from driving toward Tucson for college several times a year. In this case, though, I sped past Arizona, through Texas (God, the road was straight and endless for two entire days!), and after a few motel stops finally arrived in Pensacola. It being a sunny afternoon, I immediately headed for the beach. The sun was shining, the air cool, the waves perfect for riding, and to top it all off, there was a rock and roll band playing sanely hot music at the beach-front Pavilion.

Everybody was dancing like crazy and I joined in too, jitterbugging away. And that's when I spotted the beautiful girl. I grabbed a dance with her as she finished up her dance with a midshipman from the naval academy. In fact the place was crowded with scads of them, maybe fifty young men decked out in their freshly starched whites, all looking handsome, all wanting the next dance with this incredibly attractive, incredibly sexy, alluring young woman.

And to whom did she give her phone number

after we danced? I think what sealed the deal was when she laid her eyes on my decked-out California car—just the license plate could have won her, made her favor me over the gang of impressive-looking midshipmen.

My friend from California––call him Terry—who I'd arranged to meet there, had found me on the dance floor, and he agreed that she was a beauty. I called her up the next day and she said I could come to her house and take her out, but that I'd have to pretend I went to her high school. I said, *OK*. (So much for not being a liar, as I had so emphatically declared to the therapist!)

Now imagine me, in her living room, talking to her father and mother. He asked if I attended her high school and I said, *Yes*. Me, in my bold-faced moment. In any case, I acted the part. Is acting lying? Well, whatever it is, I passed the test enough to have her parents let me escort her out the door, promising to have her back at 11, after the movie.

Now, here's where I could have pretty much ruined my life, ended up with a statutory rape charge if my testosterone levels had been as high as some kids

I'd known, at a camp I attended in Wisconsin when I was 13. Had I been committed to seducing her I would have taken her to my motel room, and flirted with disaster. But fortunately that wasn't my intention. In any case, I hadn't been aware of the apparatus of laws set in that southern-most city, designed to protect underage kids from having sex before 18.

\

Thinking back, the first afternoon I had become a temporary resident of the Florida motel, the owner had chatted with me a little bit when I hung out around the pool, then handed me a ten-spot to buy him a six-pack of beer at the liquor store next door. I did that, returned, handed him the beer and change, and suddenly, with a strange look on his face, asked if I was 21. I said *NO*, and he gave off a little shudder. He had sent an underage kid to buy his beer.

Back to the nymph and me. Actually maybe I'm using that term inaccurately or unfairly, although she was definitely "a lovely young maiden." Nymphs were also young women who (as per Google definition) presided over various natural phenomena—from springs, to clouds, trees, caverns, meadows, and beaches. Well, she might have been able to do all that.

REAL STORY—Drive-In Date
Google goes on to say, Nymphs were not immortal, but were extremely long-lived and were, on the whole, a female deity kindly disposed toward men. That certainly fit my young and beautiful companion, now riding beside me, sitting on the tuck and roll as we headed for the nearby drive-in theater.

I don't remember the name of the movie we saw, but it wasn't because we were kissing or anything. I didn't make a move toward her, just watched the flick, and drove her back home at the scheduled time. But when we said our goodbye, standing together on the sidewalk about 200 feet from her front door, she planted a terrific kiss on my lips and pressed her pelvic region right into mine—a complete turn-on. Her smiling face, her forward kiss, beckoned me to continue our relationship, in a much more physical manner. And surely I would have, had I planned to stick around for even one more day. But my schedule dictated that I move on, head up the East Coast, to arrive in the Dedham suburb of Boston on time to join my college friend for our four-day sailboat excursion on his father's yacht, around the Cape Cod islands. So goodbye nymph!

*   *   *

BUT...what if I'd stayed on in Florida, just because I was head-over-heels in lust with the girl?

ALTERNATE UNIVERSE #2

"Hello Rick," said Mrs. Spenser, greeting me at the door for my second date with her daughter, Brenda. After a little bit of small talk (Yes, school was going good, yes. summer is fun) Brenda appeared at the top of the stairs and as she descended I'd remember later that she was every inch as incredible-looking as Cameron Diaz in the *Mask* movie with Jim Carey, that I would have seen after serving a decade in the Florida Correctional Penitentiary. Yes, that's what awaited me if I'd blinked back the legal responsibilities of dating a sixteen-year-old high school girl, letting my carnal desires rule the night.

       As Brenda slid onto the cool leather upholstery

she immediately reached over and gave me a French kiss, her tongue finding its way to mine. I was glad the key to the car was still in my hand, because if not, and the car was running, I may have inadvertently popped the clutch and ended up on a nearby lawn. Her sexuality was that powerful. I had to shake it off to proceed out of the parking space and drive accurately away.

What next? Did I really want to see the movie, she asked? I could tell that there was only one acceptable answer, but I struggled against it for just another sentence of two. "The movie is *A Hard Day's Night*. Don't you like the Beatles?"

Sure, she responded, *but you haven't shown me where you live. Maybe we could first...*

I cut her off—why, I still don't know...but maybe I kinda do.

"It's just a motel room, so unless you want to watch TV it's not the greatest..."

Without hesitation, she simply interrupted with a very bold affirmative, ultimately costing me ten years in the pen:

"That's where I want to go."

Hard to argue with the most beautiful and sensual and demanding sixteen-year-old girl-goddess that side of the Mississippi River. She had taken the fight out of me with her penetrating blue eyes, long dirty blond hair (she swished it as if controlling her own wind, Mariah), her perfect figure pressing against all sides of the fabric that covered it, and her glistening lips still wet from our kiss. *You* try resisting all that, at age 20! Needless to say, I failed.

I pulled into the Best Western Motel, gliding past the center pool, near where I had bought the beer for the owner. Of course, once inside room No. 12, and hearing she was "thirsty," it occurred to me that maybe I had one more underage beer purchase to attend to. And sure enough, the clerk didn't bat an eye as he rang up the six-pack, took my money and bagged it up.

Returning to the motel room, Brenda had turned on the TV and shed any clothes that had been uncomfortable, plus turning up the air conditioner to full blast, which I must admit delivered a kind of heavenly cool temperature to the small enclosure. She bounced around on the bed, happy as a lark, switching channels from afar, guzzling her cold beer then rolling toward me and laying another delighted kiss hard on my lips. She was just about the happiest girl I'd ever been around.

Nothing much was showing on TV—sporting events of no importance, ads for Florida beaches, real estate of some sort. She kept clicking away, and in the midst of all that her kisses came faster and with a more insistent nature. It's when she threw her whole wriggling body into the game that I went to pieces. Excuse for me getting graphic, but this is a tiny bit of what I didn't properly endure, from a legal vantage point at least.

One thing led to another, and at some point it was impossible to put on the brakes. The best analogy I can offer is this. Have you ever received a blow to the head, maybe run into a branch of a tree while riding your bike, the kind where you have blacked out for a second or two after hitting something. Suddenly there you are, flat on the ground, trying to remember what just happened and why you find yourself prone like that. Well, when I looked over at the smiling face of my young paramour, it was like coming out of a dream. There was loose clothes on the bed, her naked under the sheet, the TV rattling on, myself nude too, wet in places. The last few minutes had become a blur in my mind, but what quickly hit me was that I had no real handle on what the hell time it was. I realized that I simply couldn't afford to deliver Brenda back to her parent's house late.

I quickly glanced at the bedside motel clock radio and saw it was 10:15PM. That meant that in 15 minutes she *would* be late, although I believed that 11PM was still a forgivable time.

I rousted myself and slid on my underwear as quickly as possible, trying not to alert her or panic her in any way. Believe it or not, she was waving me in for more kissing and lovemaking. It took some doing to convince her that she now had to do two things. (1) take a quick shower and (2) get dressed and prepare for re-entry at her home. Hesitantly, with a few more kisses between us as I helped her rise off the sheets, I got her to the shower. She wasn't really drunk, just a little bit tipsy. In any case, she enjoyed my attention as I soaped up a washcloth after adjusting the water spray's temperature. She was laughing, still the most gorgeous creature I had ever laid eyes on.

Fighting the fact that everything I did for her turned her back on—toweling her dry, settling her back to sitting on the bed and getting dressed—I hopped into the shower myself for a quick soap and rinse-off. To tell the truth I was surprised to find her back in her clothes when I emerged.

Let's face it, she looked happy and basically in love with me, and that glow was an amazing thing to behold. Unfortunately, I had a disturbing grasp of hard reality to contend with. Once back in my car and rolling toward her part of town—10:55PM at this point—I tried to analyze what she needed to know about shielding us from what her parents might learn if they asked her questions about either the movie we supposedly saw, or possibly how she looked (a little bit wild and disheveled). She needed to limit her time in their presence before going to her room. It seemed I had no choice but to give her advice on what to say.

"Brenda?" I began, and she turned toward me with that same happy and trusting look. She was still feeding off the thrill of lovemaking and I realized that she had to change that for both our sakes. Here came my bucket of cold water.

"You need to be careful what you say to your parents' or you can get yourself in some trouble." I hated myself for disrupting her good mood.

"Oh...OK." she responded, dropping her energy a bit.

"Maybe try to get to bed as soon as possible, to avoid them smelling beer on your breath."

"Oh yeah, right!" She sounded like she'd handled that kind of thing before, and probably even the sex part too, since there was no blood on the sheets, or any other sign of her having been a virgin. In any case, her response made me feel a little better, about dropping her off.

She kissed me a passionate goodbye and skipped her way up to her house with abandon. That took me down a notch, since unless her parents' were zombies (they weren't) they couldn't fail to notice her happy/semi-drunk state and ask questions. As I drove away I became concerned, but by then it was obviously too late. That innocent, natural attraction I had had, to this irresistible force of nature, could easily be my undoing. That was what I had done—played with FIRE.

My vivid imagination has since filled in the gap of "What If," that is, the arrest and incarceration for rape of an underage minor in the state of Florida. Here's how it could have gone.

ALTERNATE UNIVERSE #3
(*Scary* Version)

It might have started with this—only a little different from the first rendition you just read—if I had been a somewhat normal teenager on the make, with a somewhat naive girl in my car:

"Do you want to grab a beer at my motel before the movie." She most certainly would have answered, "OK."

Since I had already purchased a six-pack the day before I have no doubt that the clerk in the liquor store would have taken my dollars again—from a now-regular customer. So, with beer, she would have been even more susceptible to making out (there was a double bed waiting to sit on, for heaven sakes, plus a TV to watch, so she did have a movie to watch, just not viewing it on an outdoor screen).

Once beers were drunk things would have

gotten out of control very rapidly, given her already impulsive and pent-up pubescent energy. It could have been a fast series of kisses, grabs, G-spot fondling, clothes being shed, penetration and the rest.

BANG, bang—someone at the door. *Oh, GOD!* Getting half-dressed minus shoes or sock I'd answer, to find myself staring down at two police officers, who brushed me aside. There, in the bed, would be my new, young sweetheart, nude, underage, scared as I was. She'd be given time to get herself properly dressed, while I sat there in a chair to the right of the TV, turned off by now by one of the cops after he saw 10 seconds of a car commercial.

After examining my driver's license (age 20), and her high school I.D. (born in 1949 = 15), they applied the cuffs to my wrists, and tried to calm down her crying as we were both escorted to the patrol cars, hers to drive her home, me for a direct ride to the station. I spotted the motel owner looking on from the picture window of his well-lit office as the vehicle rolled past, spinning red-lights causing brightly colored shadows to illuminate his face and the back walls. I'd be relieved once the patrol car had left his vicinity.

I might also get a glimpse of Brenda, as she glanced back toward me before our cars veered off in different directions.   What would her demeanor probably be, you ask? Pretty bad, like a person who had emerged from a shower and found a tornado had ripped off the roof of their house. Her face might appear younger than before, like that of a little girl, as the police were coming down on us...me. I would certainly dread what was ahead for her when delivered back to her parents in that condition. In any case, my emotions and fear of the future would quickly be directed back to my own predicament .

At the police station I'd be fingerprinted, mugshot photographed, and placed in a narrow holding cell that had just enough room for a place to sit. No water, no explanation of what would happen next.

How the hell would I explain to my mother where I was—arrested—and why. When I'd hear the charge, "Statutory Rape," it would seem so very weird, like a bad joke. She had just about raped me(!) with her sexual needs. But, of course, that was now beside the point. As the man, I was <u>the offender</u>, not her. She was the victim, and I would quickly be arraigned.

In the state of Florida the minimum charge for sex-with-a-minor, in 1964, was...12-15 years in prison. Twelve-years! Or fifteen sometimes. While I wasn't the more advanced age of a 24 male, at whom they liked to throw the book, I was still in the "20" range—so in very hot water.

Before the whole horrible experience would be over (tune in to the upcoming courtroom drama). I'd learn some history of the "Statutory Rape" offense from the high-priced attorney hired by my parents back in California. The law was enacted back in the Middle Ages, when women were considered "property" to protect. In America it had originated through English Common law, and that the age of consent was first set at age 10. Later it was raised to 18. Finally 21.

Statutory rape is considered a "liability offense," which meant that in general it didn't matter if the man did or didn't know the age of the too-young girl he had relations with. It didn't matter to the court if her appearance was older, had deceived him in any way. It all came down around the ears of the male offender.

I learned that the first successful use of the

mistake-of-age legal defense in a statutory rape case had occurred in California earlier that same year (1964) in People v. Hernandez, and that was what my lawyer would have most likely have tried (that line of defense was later revoked, and isn't a possible legal defense anymore, in 33 states, including Florida).

State to state, the "critical age of the female victim" can range from 16, to 14 (Pennsylvania), and "corruption of a minor" can sometimes be included in the charge.

In any case, I would have been in terrible trouble, if I hadn't just spent two hours at the drive-in movie and returned Brenda home by the time I had agreed to, "unmolested," Thank God there was no seduction!

I'm actually breathing a sense of relief here, realizing how close I came to the above. Playing with underage fire, as I did, could have basically ruined my life! That I ducked *that* bullet, came so close to making a wrong "dating" choice, is almost as disturbing as imagining how it would have gone for me if I'd been drafted in the 1960s into the army, given a one-way ticket to the

Vietnam jungles. Yes, life was more hazardous back then than I realized, during that life-changing "Summer of '64 in Cape Cod."

CHAPTER FOUR
Grill Chef/Vietnam

So, let me jump back to my real-life story, mid-June, 1964, as I bade the young girl (made-up name "Brenda") a kiss and watched her enter her parents house, them none the wiser that their daughter had just sat in a drive in movie with a California kid who wasn't in high school any longer!   From there, with a speedy drive up the Eastern Coast beginning the following morning, I arrived safe and sound in Boston, ready for a nice boat ride with my college friend and his Dad.

Dedham, MA, Late- June, 1964

I was warmly greeted by my friend and his mother as I was escorted into the kitchen of their house, located on one of those blocks in the Boston suburbs—you've all seen them in movies like *Good Will Hunting*, and *The Departed*. Let's call my friend "Mark," to make the story flow better. Mark's father was vice-president of a bank and had offered to take us on a trip around Cape Cod on his sailboat. I was certainly looking forward to that special outing—had never done that before. After a nice sleep on dry land, we departed the next morning.

Each day aboard ship the winds off the Cape carried us easily to the next port; Martha's Vineyard, Nantucket, and smaller destinations like the wharf of tiny Cuttyhunk were delightful experiences. A fun memory from the island (581 acres/1.5 miles long), which is considered the first English settlement in New England due to a visit there by an English ship in 1602, was being surprised by a wild turkey or two on our short hike to a church atop the center of land. Suddenly the big birds blasted out of some bushes, flapping their ineffective wings and stuttering along out of reach at an altitude of about twelve feet.

Each night Mark's father would purchase three lobsters, and that was our diet for all four boating days (I didn't complain— what a treat!).

Once back in Boston, Mark wanted to visit the Cape by car and I obliged. We headed for the beach of Martha's Vineyard, fell in with a bunch of vacationing teen girls and their adult chaperone from Hartford, Connecticut, and got to spend a lovely night with them in their rental.

After depositing Mark back at his home I

returned to Hyannis, hoping to find summer employment. I knew without income from some job I'd have to immediately cut my trip short and head back to the West Coast. I spotted a brick building on the main street with its sign, "Employment Center," and parked. Upon entering my mood dropped considerably. The place was jammed with kids around my age, all either in line with a clerk at a window, filling out forms, or in line for a restroom. And since I had to pee pretty badly, I saw that I couldn't really stand there while the line made its way to my turn.

Exiting, I spotted the hotel across the street— Hyannis Inn—and crossed over. I was pretty close to peeing in my pants so had no real choice but to try and use their facilities. I pushed open the front door and headed right in, walking with purpose through the lobby, going right by two men who were standing midway to the bathrooms, near the check-in counter. I did my business.

As soon as I was relieved I left the bathroom and headed back out. But just as I passed the same two men I heard the taller one say something like this.

"God damn dishwasher, quit right in the lunch

rush. Need another right now!"

I stopped, turned in his direction and said, "Here I am."

He glanced in my direction, and with a gruff voice asked, "Have you ever washed dishes?" I answered Yes, and that was that. He gave an order, "OK, get him back there." A young guy a couple years younger than me (maybe his son or grandson) escorted me back to the kitchen and quickly showed me the ropes—It's easy, lift the handle, roll in the rinsed glasses, lower the side down and press the green button. Same with dishes, but make them face the center sprayer—and bingo, I had my summer!

REAL STORY–Hyannis Dishwashing Gig

It had taken a miracle of timing for me to beat out all those other eager, equal-in-age-to-me local kids, but that's what had magically transpired. As the days passed, I got good at doing big pots and pans ("...feel the surfaces while washing," I'd been instructed), as well as keeping up with the usual piles of plates, silverware, glasses and cups from the mealtimes. And it felt like I was part of a family, since each day the help like me, including waitress and cooks, were served a full-course lunch, prepared specially by the main chef. Great food; ham, turkey, beef, chicken with all the trimmings, appeared as if by magic. Free food and $52.50 a week. And I had never eaten better.

Did I mention free lodging as well? Actually, probably only the pre-adult males like me, pre-twenty, anyway, would have appreciate sleeping on mattresses on a basement floor, underneath one of the rented cabins. Privacy was maintained with blankets hanging from rafters to separate each small sleeping quarters. But with those necessities covered, every cent of my paycheck went right into my wallet. And I needed cash to repair the blown head gasket I'd suddenly acquired since becoming employed. Fortunately, I had enough tools along to remove the carburetors, valve covers, valves (I kept them numbered for replacement), finally pulling the head and getting it machined nearby.

Another bonus of working at the Inn was that I got to meet young waitresses my own age, with one of them becoming my summer girlfriend. We'd travel in my car in the evenings after work (after 10PM) once I got it running, and park out on the coastal road

(Chappaquiddick couldn't have been much further down the road), and listen to the radio, kiss, talk, without her allowing anything beyond our petting going on. The friendship felt nice and I somehow didn't really miss the sex part (still hadn't had that kind of fully physical relationship with a member of the opposite sex, so you could say I didn't know what I was missing!).

So there was basically a complete and new life-cycle for me, formed those 3000+ miles from home. I had employment—pretty stress-free—definitely a lot more pleasurable than hitting my head against a wall to get grades for a professional career in aeronautical engineering. Plus food and shelter as I've mentioned, new friends and even a gaining respect from the head chef and owner of the place.

At a point when I informed the head chef that I'd be departing home to California in a couple weeks, returning to college and all, I was offered a permanent job by Chef Claude (another made-up name), who said he wanted to train me as a "grill chef." I was flattered, but declined, since I had to go back to finish up my studies.

It was probably a good thing that I hadn't fully understood what a big deal it was, to be offered a position as a real chef in a real and noted restaurant, at age 20. I was being given a chance to break into a career of that sort, something that's very hard to come by, even if you are a top student at some culinary institute. And this wasn't some dinky. no-nothing kitchen at a no-nothing restaurant. When I'd first started washing dishes there I'd been told, probably by the kid who showed me around, that Bobby Kennedy and his family had just eaten there the week before. I'd seen the Kennedy compound off in the distance across the water when I'd lazed about the beach between shifts, after clearing dishes from the lunch crowd.

So how did I suddenly fall into favor with these professionals? Number one, I was incredibly grateful for the job and I had applied myself 100%. I'd done an immaculate job of making sure everything that passed through my hands was spotlessly clean. You would have laughed to see the huge pile of pots and pans that sat to one side of my sink after each meal. I scrubbed away at these large items—felt the surfaces with my fingers—never passed anything on that had food stuck to it,

Then, after the washing work was done, my extended duties were to cleaning the kitchen, mopping the entire floor, checking around the stoves, large ovens, counters, to remove any food debris. I was shown how to mop and clean efficiently, and was completely effective if I do say so myself.

Soon, I got faster at the cleanup, and found each afternoon that I still had about an extra hour left on the clock. Since I had no desire to just sit on my hands and twiddle my thumbs, look stupid and lazy, I invented a job they hadn't instructed me on. I'd noticed that there was a lot of filth along the floor, right under all the counters, a buildup of dirt and old food debris that never got addressed. And I quickly understood why no one had bothered. Not even the water and soap from mopping removed it . So each day during the last month of my job, I tackled that grime, attacked about a foot of floor-space per session, scrapping with a chisel-like tool, then using a thick SOS-type wire ball, adding some elbow-grease to clean away the unsightly messes. And slowly, deliberately, I carved my way around the room. I never imagined that someone may have noticed what I was doing, but probably the head chef (possibly even the ornery owner) were impressed.

Another bonus of the job was being pulled aside by the chef and taught how to make their special clam chowder in a very tall pot. It was a step-by-step instruction—this many clams into a mixture of so-much milk after I'd semi-fry and add bacon bits in the bottom. I laughed to myself, knowing that their lowly dishwasher was preparing the "Famous Hyannis Inn Chowder" for customers.

Another skill I was taught during my dishwashing stint was descending to the basement, entering the freezer and identifying and grabbing certain cuts of meat for the chef—big cuts of beef, sirloin, flank, filet mignon, all the while being instructed on the different cuts when they were in that frozen state. One day I was given the task of separating the Maine lobsters from the "chicken" lobsters, having been cautioned that they could take a finger off with their claws if I wasn't careful.

Another interesting thing that happened during my short dishwashing career was when I made a young customer happy with a free desert. I was re-stocking clean plates in the middle ante-room, where waitresses dash in and out through swinging doors to grab cooked dinners off the counter and served them to diners. I had spotted the little girl in that small space and was impressed that she had somehow passed through the swinging door from the main dining room side, escaped her family. Anyway, she was tearful, and I couldn't help asking her what was wrong. Whatever it was, she couldn't seem to put it into words. Since it was a Sunday, and the rules for kitchen help like me were that I could make myself "one dessert a week," I decided to use my treat-power to make her happy. "Like ice cream?" I asked. That got a nod and a lessening of tears.

I then definitely held her attention by scooping out a big ball of vanilla ice cream into a tall sundae glass (there was a handy freezer with frozen desserts, tall cake rack, where waitresses could quickly answer dessert orders). She brighten up considerably as I added the second scoop, poured in hot chocolate sauce, squirted on whip cream and dropped a cherry on top. Needless to say, her bad mood disappeared, as she set upon devouring it, her smiling lips soon spotted with chocolate and cream. She took it through the swinging door and disappeared. But before I could exit the room the boss was on me, chewing me out.

"What the hell..." he stuttered. "You...WE don't give food away. We sell it. Don't ever do that again!"

A few waitresses witnessed this, gracing me with wide smiles—giving credit for my daring to risk an interaction with the owner.

*   *   *

So. all along, I was being groomed for future kitchen work, and didn't realize it—valued enough to be forgiven for unsanctioned sundae-making! Only later, much later and long gone from that opportunity, did I realize that I could have become a player-of-sorts in the big-time culinary business, with a great resume entry concerning my chef work at a well-established restaurant where something like 120 lunches and upwards of 200 dinners were served each day.

Imagining it now, 50+ years later, I would have been at the top of the earning curve, responsible for expertly cooking the most expensive meats for their sometimes illustrious customers. That's what I walked away from. And I have to wonder why I did, given the uncomfortable and uninspiring college life that awaited. Why didn't I just grab that offer like a drowning man thrown a life preserver? Why didn't I start earning a real wage around people who appreciated me? I was all set to have a new, quite pleasurable existence. I have no good answer, other than that I was and always have been "a finisher," someone who keeps at things until I reach the finish-line. College wasn't completed yet.

But still, how did I intuitively know that what appeared to be a perfect choice—becoming a well-paid chef in that sweet Cape Cod town—was completely wrong for me? Of course, now I know what was at stake, but back then I would have had to have been clairvoyant to see a possible future that awaited—being drafted into the army for Vietnam for one thing. Had I cooked instead of attending college, I could have ended up crawling around in horribly humid jungle, fighting for survival! So, that seemingly innocent career choice—grill chef in Cape Cod—could have dished up a tremendous shift in my fate.

But first, please enjoy this fictional account of the pleasurable beginning of that life as a chef, which was certainly possible if I had just blinked during my short time in beautiful Cape Cod, 1964.

*   *   *

ALTERNATE UNIVERSE #4

The phone call to my mother was a disruptive one. I knew my decision to drop out of college would be disappointing.

"But honey, you were starting to do so well—good...or better grades. Didn't that feel good?"

"Yes...I guess so. (Pause) But I just wasn't confident that I really knew anything. The grades were OK, but the stuff I was being graded on just fell right out of my head afterwards. Not really learning anything I would ever actually use...to build a bridge or send a rocket to the moon."

(Silence on the phone, so I continued.)

"Here, at the restaurant, I understand things,

and what they teach me is sticking with me. In my brain. I even do their clam chowder—what Bobby Kennedy will maybe order next time he comes in."

"Bobby Kennedy eats there?"

"Yeah. He did. They said so. With his family, a week ago, before my job began. They say I'll be taught the job of a grill chef, so I'll be earning pretty good money, and learning something."

"Well I...(I could hear her softening). Maybe it is for the best. So, they are nice people?"

"Yep. The head chef has been teaching me all about meat cuts—I get the frozen roasts and lobster tails out of the fridge downstairs. He says he will help me do this."

"Well, I guess you might as well try it then. (*Yay, no more school!*)

"You can always return back to college in a semester if it doesn't work out. I'll explain it to dad. He may even be impressed with the Kennedy connection. Must be a pretty good restaurant..."

"Thanks Mom! I'll call again to say how it's going!"

Getting off the phone I felt a big sense of relief. I could stay there in Hyannis, do my nice, stress-free job instead of reading complicated books and listening to teachers talk about confusing things. Engineering classes were very complicated and now I was free of all that. Wow! Maybe I could finally be happy.

The chef, Claude, seemed pleased that I would take his offer, though he didn't give off any more emotion than usual. As he started to explain what I would be undertaking—how the grill was turned on, how to set the temperature, and requirements for the different meats—he continued to smoke his cigarettes, deposit them on the different counters still lit, as before. I think I counted ten cigarettes burning away the last time he walked me through something he was explaining, before he suddenly freaked out when he realized that the baked potatoes were getting overcooked. While I was standing beside him he suddenly flipped open the long pizza-oven type lid and grabbed the rack of potatoes—maybe 15 of them on a pie tin—and pulled them out, setting it down on the counter, all with his bare hands! He tried to soft-pedal the burning of his hands, conceal that from me, but it was obvious that that had been a very bad and impulsive decision. Hopefully, I would always remember to use oven mitts when necessary.

The first thing Claude said after I agreed to stay on was, "We need to get you a place to live." I nodded. "Somewhere close by, so you can be in here quickly, no traveling. I think I know a good place."

OK, is all I said. I wasn't really used to chatting away with him, so I went back to my cleaning duties and looked forward to living somewhere other that on the floor in the basement of Cottage #2.

Later that day, during our evening together in my car, parking along the shore and enjoying the sound of waves in the distance, the fresh ocean air, I had to explain to my waitress girlfriend that I couldn't now drive her and her girlfriends back to the Midwest, because I was staying on, going to be a chef there. She was pretty understanding—a nice girl that I had been happy to know. We kissed some more, as usual, and in a sense it was a bunch of goodbye kisses rolled together, one last smooch at her doorstep. Never heard from her again.

So while I was waiting to get an apartment, Claude began my preparation for the cooking job. First-off he gave me three days with pay for just watching the other fry and grill chefs doing their jobs. The new pay, $95 per week to start, was almost double the $51 I'd been earning by cleaning dishes.

"Just talk to me for a couple minutes each day and tell me what you see," said Claude. "It's a good way to learn," he added. "And don't get bothered by the other kids who work here. They can act tough around newcomers. Like a pecking order."

I discovered pretty quickly that the "homeys," the chefs I was hired to join, were residents there in Hyannis and were the same ones who had teased me earlier, calling me College, as in, "Hey College, want a pork chop?" In that earlier case, one of the mid-twenties grill chefs had flung a cooked chop across the room to me and I had caught it with one hand and taken a bite while my other hand was on the controls of the dishwashing machine. It wasn't surprising to me when they continued teasing me about coming from dishwashing.

"Hey, dish-man, sure you ready for the hot

stove?" said Jimmy, the kid of 24 who I was set to replace. Claude had told me I was being hired because they needed a fill-in, since one of the cooks had decided to go in the military. Jimmy was a thin-faced young guy, with a light beard peeking out on his cheeks, a somewhat ruddy complexion, brown hair (kept in a net while he cooked, it looked like a bird's nest). He stood taller than me, by maybe two inches, and wore old jeans under his apron. He'd been the pork chop-tosser that month back. Probably wouldn't eat anything like that again, but I liked the way the other two guys got a kick out of my participation with Jimmy's little game.

So, goodbye Jimmy. Actually there was almost something "military" about him already, come to think of it. He had a proper stiffness, like he was already someone who had marched in line, stood at attention, then gone "at ease" on command. Anyway, like other uninformed youth of the early 60s, I didn't realize what Jimmy was walking into, and wished him luck before he shipped off. At least I'd broken the ice with him, been "one of the kitchen guys," so he and the others––Don Jr. and Sammy––those locals who delivered the steaks, boiled lobsters, sandwiches to the waitresses through a large window, didn't seem to mind me hanging around too much.

Quickly I absorbed the routine from the grill's perspective. The waitresses would hear the little "ding" of the counter bell, signaling hot food was up—the service window could hold six big dinner plates at a time. The chefs had fun making up code names relating to each order, often ones with a sexual connotation (which the young waitresses seemed to get a kick out of). Most of the girls who worked there were around the cooks same age, some pretty attractive, some not so much, but all of them, skinny-tall, fat-slim, blond-brunette, seemed to have a fun-and-feisty nature, just like the chefs.

As my paid three-days rolled on, I learned to appreciate this little dance between the cooks, the waitresses, while also getting a sense of how long certain cuts of meat took to broil, to conditions from rare-to medium, and just plain done. The success of the restaurant depended on these twenty-something local kids, who could work fast and efficiently, and it tickled me that I would soon also be one of those. I was glad I could be brought up to speed by watching them do their thing, hearing their banter, their mouthing off, flirting, and ultimately delivering top-notch dinners. The waitresses each gave me a little nod as I tagged along on the hot stove side of the counter—a wink here, a smile there gave me a nice feeling.

When I'd been their dishwasher, just days earlier actually, they'd noticed how I'd gotten in trouble with the boss for giving a crying little girl a free chocolate Sunday, and that had given me some big points. I remembered a certain pretty waitress who passed by to get her orders and how she had snuck me a beautiful, life affirming grin. She had been delighted at my antics. So with that memory, I felt confident that I had produced some good will within the tight-knit year-around waitress cadre.

At the end of the first-day dinner shift, around 10:45PM, chef Claude pulled me aside and said, "Can we talk?" *Sure.* He walked me over to an outside couple of table and chairs where we sat down. The late August night was warm and balmy, with a hint of ocean in the air.

"What did you learn, Rick?" he quickly asked, not wasting any time waiting for results from my paid observing.

"Well, I saw that the grill was crowded with steaks and that Jimmy spent time sliding the meat from left to right after he pulled them from the broiler. I guess that kept them warm, but not overcooked. On a few, he left his spatula under a steak. Guessing that kept it even more carefully warm, but not cooking anymore.

"Right," said Claude, a little smile accompanying his word. "You have to make sure that the food is piping hot when it's delivered to the waiting plate—those dinners must go hot right to a waitress. "OK. What else?"

"I watched as Jimmy pressed down on the steaks with his long cooking fork, and he explained that as a future grill guy I needed to watch for when the juice changes from red to clear color. That's when the meat goes from rare and medium rare to medium."

Claude was nodding as I said all this.

"Jimmy told you right. Working the grill, a chef has to be instantly aware of when the meat hits that point. If someone orders a filet cooked "medium" then you keep it on the grill until it's leaking clear fluid, then remove it immediately and let it rest on the rack so it doesn't dry out while you load the baked potato or fries or mashed, and vegetable of the day.

"We're going to miss Jimmy—a good kid...like you. Have a good evening, and we'll talk tomorrow. Feel free to join us for some dinner later"

It was nice to feel appreciated, and Claude gave me a good feeling about myself. I reminded myself to ask Jimmy a couple questions about his joining up in military service when I saw him the next day. In any case, I hung around for a few more minutes, just walking the kitchen, acknowledging the other guys who I'd get to know better—their wisecracks not too bothersome.

As I rounded a corner near the front, near the salad bar and desert-making counters, I almost bumped into the waitress who had watched me make the little girl's dessert. She said, "Hi," and without missing a beat, adding, "I'm Rita, as in *Hayworth*. Want to be beaten in golf later?"

I gave a chuckle, and replied, "Of course,"

adding, "except I don't have clubs, or shoes, or balls."
(I thought about the balls comment later, with all its
funny implications).

"I don't mean the real kind, silly. *Miniature*
golf. Just down the street. Meet me at 10:15 tonight
and I'll whip your ass! At "Jones's."

OK, was the only thing to say. "I'll be there."

"Good, Grill man."

And she disappeared after stacking her arm with
four plates off the counter and exiting through the
swinging door into the restaurant. She was a lovely,
obviously adroit blond (all those plates!), with a big
smile to boot, and it was impossible to say *no.*

I didn't have to wait even a minute at the Main
Street entrance of Jones' Miniature Golf before she ran
up. "Hi, victim. Lets do some putting. My treat."

She had a flashy way about her, her body-
language assured, with a spunky energy that indicated
she was pretty athletic.

"So you live in Hyannis full-time?" I said,
curious to say the least.

"Yeah, just another townie who couldn't get
into college, college boy."

"Ha!" I laughed.   She seemed to know everything about me. As she handed me the putter after paying she added, "Not everybody picks grungy kitchen work over college, but you're forgiven." (Another lovely smile sent my way.)

"Let's get those balls rolling. Got an early shift tomorrow."

So we putted from one hole to another, and she was pretty good, winning many with her shots. Up embankments, and down, curving around, sending her ball up ramps into clown mouth-holes, beating out the pendulum obstacles, ricocheting off the sides to make holes in one or two. She'd lived in town long enough to know how to conquer each obstacle.

"Nice game," she said, adding, "Got some balls at my apartment—meat balls—and noodles.   So, hungry?"

Yes I was. Her walk-up studio was just a block away. We climbed the stairs, she leading the way. and I continued to notice how beautiful she was from every angle. Inside we shed our coats, and before I ever saw a meat ball she kissed me, I kissed back, and our clothes dropped away almost instantly. I woke up in her bed just as she was sliding her jeans over her lovely legs.

"Just relax, sleepyhead. Someone has to work in this family!" With another great kiss planted firmly on my lips she was out the door. Needless to say, I was now happier than ever that I'd stayed put at the Hyannis Inn.

That afternoon I was back at the kitchen, talking to Jimmy, and touching base with the other young chefs I'd be working with after Jimmy was gone. When it was just Jimmy and me I had to ask him about his decision to enlist.

"How come the military, Jimmy. Seems like you had it good here?"

"I donno. Been here for three years, and seemed like a rut. No fun. At least in the Marines you get buffed out—strong muscles—and get respect. And good pay too, even college money if I ever want to goof off...like you've done!" He added that "goofed off" part with a laugh, and I had to agree that for most college kids it was just fooling around. But with engineering classes, like what I took, you hardly got to see daylight since each problem took many hours to solve. For the first four problems in the back of my Statics and Dynamics engineering book I'd been stymied, spending eight hours on #1, then finally just giving up. That's when I decided to mostly stop attending classes (blackboards the teacher filled up each class session, with vector calculus which I hadn't even had yet, was infuriating), and just take the tests almost blindly. My method for studying for tests was that I just reviewed the sample problems in the book—12 examples—going back over them endless times. Surprisingly, I had received a 35% on the big midterm test, and that equaled a solid "C" since it was graded on the curve. Still, that ended all my good feelings about my Aeronautical Engineering career. I couldn't really believe that I should be trusted to keep a satellite up in the atmosphere.

Jimmy said he was a little scared about being in a war, but added that nothing much was happening then (Fall, 1964) except for some pajama-clad Vietnamese peasants doing an uprising over there. I told him I knew what he meant, having seen some images like that in my ROTC college class in Arizona. I didn't bother to say how stupid it felt marching around at

7AM for that class, because I didn't have to take that military experience seriously. Just a stupid requirement, with fraternity kids acting like soldiers, being "squad leaders," most a bunch of arrogant jerks bossing us all around. Hopefully, the real military wasn't like that. Jimmy told about his father and uncle serving in Korea, and that, he said, was a real fuckin' war. His uncle had lost a leg. But they were proud he'd signed up. He said he'd send me a postcard, to me at the kitchen sometime, from Hanoi (wherever that was).

Back to cooking, he demonstrated boiling lobsters, showing how to keep clear of any pinching claws once the rubber bands were removed. And he revealed the secret of making stuff he cooked taste good.

"Garlic butter. That's what we do for steaks, lobsters, shrimp, garlic bread of course, everything! That, and a little salt and pepper and no one complains. The customers are happy." I nodded as he added with a laugh, "...even Kennedy and their kids cleaned their plates!"

"Have you actually seen them...when they're in

the dining room?   Or just the waitresses while serving..."

"Yeah, cause sometimes they've asked to meet us cooks when the food was good.   We'd get autographs and stuff.   He seems like an OK guy...Robert. The kids are just normal kids too, just a lot of them at the two tables we move together."

Seemed like Jimmy enjoyed being my teacher, maybe even a future friend. I said I'd check back later and headed for the beach for my break, to get some air and maybe a tan.   Wherever Rita was, if we didn't cross paths in the sand I'd find her at the dinner rush later. It was hard to believe how easily and quickly I now had a girlfriend as well as a good-paying job. Call it getting two new families, in about that same amount of days. And soon a home of my own, some apartment that Claude knew was coming up for rent. Lucky me, to have someone looking out for my interests.

Before I forget, Chef Claude said that in his kitchen I had to think of doing every thing *in threes*. When I hesitated to respond he explained the concept in more detail.

"Say you're chopping some onion for a stew or

as garnish for a steak. What I'm saying is, *chop, chop, chop*. That means you chop the onion three times, maybe another three times, but *not* in two-chops or a single *chop*. This rule saves time, and money. This way, you don't get stalled with any job in the kitchen. If you're cooking a burger you can flip it once to get the underside better cooked. If you doubt that side-one is fully cooked, then flip it back there one more time, no more. Stir the soup pot three times and put down the spoon."

I guess I was looking in Claude's direction with a bit of daze in my eyes, because he quickly finished up.

"Just give the Three Times Only rule a try.

"Thanks Rick. See you tomorrow."

And he exited out the side door, past the bakery where all the delicious blueberry muffins were baked at 5AM each morning. I used to drop in for a free hot muffin after my date with an earlier waitress girlfriend from Michigan. Yum!

I'd heard the other kitchen workers complaining about the high rents in Hyannis and how some of them even had to drive into work from the mainland, near Boston proper, saying that the gas money was obviously eating into their paychecks. So there were things I didn't as yet know about my new grill life. But my new opportunity was clearly what I'd always wanted—to start fresh at something that I was good at—and I'd never gotten that kind of chance before. Let's call it receiving respect, appreciation, even love (thanks now to my blazing relationship with Rita). Of course, I didn't see the bombshells coming. Mainly, if you'weren't in college you could be drafted in those years. (And that's where I'll end this Rita/Grilling chef fantasy!)

*   *   *

So, in real life NO VIETNAM! Never served! Since I didn't accept Claude's offer of cooking in Hyannis Port, I was temporarily protected from becoming a 1-A draftee by returning to college. But what if I hadn't?

ALTERNATE UNIVERSE #5

If I had been drafted (having thrown my 1-A letter in the garbage and just forgetting about it, like I'd actually done in real life in Arizona), it could have gone something like this:

Here's an account I wrote about arriving in Vietnam—feet on the ground—from ducking bullets on the tarmac to being knocked unconscious by a blast that took one of my legs. I used a made-up name, "Rudy," for this chapter-length fiction that appeared in my first novel, <u>Black President</u> (Picnic Books, UK, ©2008), and I feel it gives a pretty realistic taste of what the military experience could have been like for me. It helps me to get some distance on what would surely have been a very traumatic experience. Try to imagine yourself as the character, Rudy, as he is suddenly immersed in jungle warfare.

<u>Vietnam War, 1965</u>
On the flight to Vietnam from the holding base on Okinawa, Rudy enjoyed the air conditioning and the free meal, but when they came in sight of Da Nang he heard some of the men talking about other planes taking flak. He had already learned from others at Okinawa about the fifty-yard dash from the plane to the airport buildings. The thirteen-monthers who had

returned alive painted a pretty grim picture. They said some of their men had been blown away before they'd barely got off the plane, so Rudy asked to be issued his rifle and flak jacket on the plane, but that didn't happen. Luckily the incoming rounds were at a temporary halt as his plane finally touched down.

When the door was cracked opened for disembarkment, Rudy and his fellow recruits were overwhelmed by the intensity of the heat that invaded the cabin. Soon they were marching out, hup-hup fashion, and headed over to a big quonset hut where salt tablets were dispensed.

"Take two of these fuckers every day," instructed the young lieutenant, "And I mean TWO," emphasized the officer. "Or you'll probably get heatstroke and die on your own, before the VC can get you. And we don't want no suicides around here, OK?"

After a quick role call each man was issued his M-16. Things were happening fast, thought Rudy. This is a no-shit op. It took only twenty minutes to hand out weapons and assign men to their base.

"You...Tempers. You're Second Division. That's Quang Tri. Tomorrow, 0800."

"Yessir," said Rudy, happy that there was still time to hit the Da Nang streets with his buddies. And things appeared pretty civilized, as jungle towns went. The military men Rudy passed on the sidewalks were still keeping up their appearance—creased pants, spit-shined boots, clean uniforms—carrying themselves along with a certain bravado. In comparison to U.S. soldiers, though, the local people looked ragged, shabby, and always in a hurry. The dirty babies playing in what looked like sewer water, didn't help the image. Not a pretty sight. And Quang Tri was definitely a step down from there. Many more ramshackle houses, more ragged people, kids running around half-naked, more garbage and sewer water everywhere he looked. But there was no time to get fixated, because orders kept him moving.

Next it was on to Phu Bai. Rudy knew he would forget some of the names when he tried to write Rita a postcard. He still kept in touch with his best girl. He had come to realize that if she had just become pregnant back when they were together, he would never have gotten drafted in the first place.

"Tango-Two" was his new company. And they kept shifting Rudy to new locations. After breakfast at 0530 they loaded him and other new recruits onto a truck and headed for "LZ Stud"—a real squirrely place he'd heard—with the ground all torn up and only bunkers and hooches for defense. It didn't take long to see some badly impaired people hanging around. Rat bites on faces and arms, infected wounds, bodies just waiting to be removed. Things were turning nightmarish fast. Yeah, he thought, I should have got married. Rita had said NO, because she said "freedom was sexier." Crazy girl! But then I would have had only a wife and a mother-in-law to put up with.

Next, it was Khe Sanh, and all pretext of an orderly military operation dissolved. None of the soldiers Rudy spotted on the ridge or along the trench line even bothered to wear the stripes anymore. And in the mid-morning it looked like the men had just woke up, rolled out of bed and forgotten to tuck in their shirts or shave. But the sargeants still played the game, yelled orders and hustled the men along, splitting them up, assigning them to different parts of the mountain. The oppressive heat wore Rudy down, so that his pack felt like double its sixty-pound weight. He stripped it off as soon as the platoon neared the barbed wire, just dumped it off his shoulder. Lots of other men followed his lead.

Next, the squad leader ordered Rudy and some others to don their jungle fatigues, but since none had been issued, the men just made do as best they could, tearing off sleeves, cutting pants into shorts. Some Marines already stationed there threw in extra t-shirts and rags that somehow became usable clothing. The scene looked like a crazy, out-of-control garage sale. Within minutes, two other young Marines walked up and handed Rudy clothes they had discarded. An oversized shirt was handed to him from a black guy named "Ruffy." Nothing about Ruffy's wardrobe was regulation. He wore a red bandana around his forehead to hold back his Afro, and his T-shirt had a big "R" painted across it with some kind of red ink or paint, the crusty lines lifting off the fabric. Cut-off blue jean shorts completed Ruffy's "uniform." The dogtags that said "Military" were there on a chain, but he could just have easily been heading for a spring break at Fort Lauderdale.

Rudy's pants came from a thin White guy in his early twenties, who called himself "Shadow." Rudy figured the name was because the guy dressed in black and had black face paint smeared under his eyes and across his forehead

"For the glare," Shadow announced, when noticing Rudy's odd expression. "Gooksville warpaint," he added, "To spook them fuckers."

Before Shadow turned and walked away, he threw his hunting knife straight into the ground, less than a foot away from Rudy's foot. "Cut the legs off if you want to." Shadow took two steps, turned and, pointing at the knife spoke again with a laugh.

"Too bad I missed your foot – coulda been your plane ticket to Hawaii."

Within the hour, Rudy was ordered to jump in a bunker. That's where he'd be living...where the gunners were positioned. It was tough easing himself down into that dark hole in the ground, really just an underground mud hut. Where are the rats? he wondered. He'd been told that the rats were exceptionally big and aggressive around there, and that he should show no mercy if he spotted one. Luckily, none showed their ugly mugs that first day. Later on it wouldn't matter, to him or anyone stationed there, because killing rats and other things (whatever moved) became necessary sport to staying alive.

Within the next hour, Rudy heard the squad leader shout, "High haunches, you mothers!"

There was no time to think. Rudy was soon running around with an M-16, somewhere in the jungle. When someone spotted a dead VC, sprawled in the bushes with his guts spilled out, the squad leader called for Rudy to come over. Rudy took a quick look, breathed in the rotten smell and immediately threw up, vomiting his lunch. The squad leader, nicknamed "Frisky," gave the next order. He wanted the dead man's intestines to be pulled out and stretched between two trees. They could be thirty feet long, he said, and wanted them measured.

"You got to be kidding," said Rudy, but Frisky just stared at him, humorlessly. He wasn't kidding. Frisky said something about sticking fingers inside a body to warm stiff hands. Rudy tried to approach the body again, and puked some more. Finally he managed to grab the intestines and start pulling. He felt the warmth—it was true. He tugged some more and suddenly the whole mess gushed out. Rudy staggered back, bent over dry-heaving. Again he faced the task, grabbed the intestines and started walking, one step, two steps.

It only took two hours for Rudy's indoctrination into death to be complete. All the new guys got a similar lesson. The enemy dead was nothing to cry over. They're hardly human. Killing them was good, like removing an insignificant pest from off the kitchen floor. Just bring your foot down hard and stomp, shoot, stab, hack them without mercy. Then sweep the crap away.

Rudy learned quickly from the old-timers that the real warriors picked prizes off the dead. Out would come their knives, and they'd carve off the ears, noses, stringing the VC mementos on their hat band or belt loop. And if you didn't do that, didn't deface the corpses, your Phoenix buddies would seriously wonder if you had a problem.

Go on. Cut off a few ears for souvenirs, they'd prompt. You earned it.   Maybe even a penis or breast...like Rudy saw Shag do. Shag was another of the long-timers. Shag didn't give a fuck. It would be much later, after Rudy got half blown apart, that he would wonder what all his buddies did with the beef-jerky ears after they got home. Did they hide them in envelopes in their trunks, back in New York, Kansas, Georgia, Utah, Colorado, or California? Thousands of dried-up ears and other body parts were waiting to be found across the U.S. That future lawyer, accountant, doctor, businessman, gas station attendant had killed people without mercy. What if their wives, kids, girlfriends, mothers, buddies back home ever found out all the truth?

Frisky was a "Phoenix" operative. That's the Op the top guys worked for. Rudy was told it was an intelligence program–CIA foreign—that was trying to knock off the VC leadership. There was hardly anyone in it past twenty-years-old, except for old-man Frisky. And he was "twenty-mother-fuckin'-four." Frisky said if Rudy did real good he could be recruited too.

And like everyone else at Khe Sanh, Rudy hit the weed, the LSD tabs and brew, and waited for assignments So, death to gooks. No big deal. Just wipe 'em out. Collect your trophies. But if a Marine got killed...now that was something tragic. When they murdered one of your brothers, one of your own, it was time to get even...even times two. That's all Frisky had to say. He'd yell, TIMES TWO! Everybody knew what he meant. Kill every fucking thing that moved. Entire villages got wiped out.

Rudy repeatedly stuck his hands inside dead Vietnamese bodies and felt his fingers loosen up. In fact, it became his trademark. Everyone had one. Rudy remembered that feeling of dipping his fingers into hot oil back at the service station where he worked as a kid, digging out an oil pan plug during oil changes. Not much different. Bloody Rudy, said Shag. Red Hands Rudy, someone else joked. RHR, Frisky chimed. Others joined with Ra...har...Ra...har. And the name stuck.

Watch out for Rahar! He's one crazy, mother fuckin' jar-head!

And did you ever hear Rahar roar? When Rudy took

down a village, aced the population, Rahar really roared.

October 24, 1965.

When the village just outside of LoDuc was called up on the screen, Rahar's Op was told to "Terminate with extreme prejudice." Given the need for body count and the presence of suspected VC, the order wasn't unusual. The fog hung low in the air that morning, a tunnel of vision below a pillowy, off-white overcast. Three re-cons crawled forward and scoped out the turf that was in the proximity of the rice fields, while Rahar, Frank and Dandy-D eased into position, rifles, grenades and knives at hand. They figured on a messy assault and needed to be ready. Besides, Dandy-D had a good collection of scalps to maintain, so a sharp knife was a must, he mumbled, cheerily.

At 0800 the first strafing jets laid down a tidy line of napalm behind the village, along the treeline. Some good scorching there, thought Rudy as he hoisted up his M-16 and moved in quickly with his buddies. Rat-tat-tat, rat-tat-tat. Chu-chu-chu. The sound of rifles firing and explosives detonating was heard in all directions. What a rush, thought Rudy. Better than any drug.

Kill anything that moved. That was the order of the day. Click them out. That's all it was. Patoo-patoo and an old man to the left was nearly cut in half by Rahar's happy fire. But no time to inspect.

"Move in! Move in! " someone yelled, and they did, clicking out the old, young, male and female—no prejudice. Rahar ducked into a hooch and started firing before he looked. Good safety measure. No time to draw and shoot like in the old west. If there was someone inside, then they were, by definition, VC. So click them out.

The old woman twitched as she fell against the straw wall, dropping something from her hands as she went down. A sack of rice hit the floor and Rahar kicked it out of his way. The bag bounced against the central hearth of the hooch, then stopped. Rahar focused down and spotted the baby, there in the dirt near where it landed. Some kind of human feeling emerged, from way back in the recesses his mind, and made him reach out to test for life. But he never reached the bundle. The excruciating pain in his side spun him around, firing wildly as he dropped. His rounds caught the baby's father across the face, as Rahar slammed unconscious into the hard-pack.

Like I said earlier, Vietnam never happened. And neither did a full-time grill chef job on Cape Cod—Jimmy didn't teach me how garlic butter brushed on various meats and seafoods improves the taste, because he wasn't real And there was no beautiful lovemaking with anyone named "Rita," the waitress who found my chocolate Sunday-making for the little girl so endearing. These characters only exist as part of my "Alternate Universe."

REAL STORY—Back To College

I had just done the normal thing, the expected thing—had gotten in my '58 Plymouth, started it up, the two carburetors frantically sucking in gas, loaded in the three Michigan waitresses, two in the back, one shotgun, filled the trunk with their suitcases—I hadn't even had enough clothes that summer to half-fill a

paper bag—and left the Cape in the dust.   Still
wondering why I picked pain—*pain over pleasure*
(earning money by being effortlessly good at
something=pleasure), instead of returning to college to
continue being a lousy student.   Some things like this
must continue to remain mysterious, I guess.

The "Michigan" waitresses (remember, one of
them was my sort-of girlfriend from the Inn) asked if
we could travel by way of a stop in New York City,
where one of them had access to her uncle's tiny
Manhattan studio apartment.. I remember two main
things about that overnight stay in the Big Apple.
(One) The women had no problem prancing around the
small room in their underwear—bras and panties
everywhere in my eyesight.   Pretty funny that my
maleness wasn't any kind of a threat to their "letting it
all hang out," so to speak.   (Two) Within the nice
apartment—the view of Manhattan spread out beyond
the windows was intoxicating—there was a little
second room, an office where the wall was completely

covered with framed photos of the waitress's uncle with celebrities, one of which was Marilyn Monroe. I guess he must have been an entertainment lawyer, an agent or something. So I enjoyed the novelties of that visit.

Anyway, aside from the Plymouth's engine running out of oil half way across Ohio and me pouring three oil cans worth back in—luckily I had cans stored in the trunk—I efficiently returned the three riders to their homes and, in one case, into the hands of her boyfriend. I remember that when I dropped off the prettiest of the waitresses, at a crossroads somewhere outside of Ann Arbor—just a farmhouse and a barn was in the distance— her boyfriend, who was standing there, planted a big kiss on her lips then gave me a dirty, jealous look, like I'd been screwing her or something. A funny "territorial" moment. The second girl had also been dropped off with her friend there, so the jealous boyfriend had two women around. At any rate, from there I headed toward my summer girlfriend's home in Ann Arbor proper. I got to spend the night at her parents house (back to Michigan

University it was for her, a Latin major). They wished me well, a nice ride home after giving me a hearty breakfast, and around mid-morning I jumped back in my ride and hauled ass back toward my home on the Wear Coast.

I drove pretty continuously, not stopping for hotels or anything because I had very little money left at that point. I was mainly concerned that the few dollars I had in my wallet wouldn't buy enough gas to reach my destination. Luckily, back then I was able to get gallons for nineteen cents. Remember, it was 1964, with gas and cigarettes very cheap—cancer-sticks also 19 cents a pack!

I rolled into my Santa Barbara driveway with barely a quarter tank left, hit the sack, woke up, talked to mom, ate some food, and then heard that my ailing father wanted to go over my classes with me on the sun porch. He was very ill, then on oxygen for his emphysema, and he gulped for breath as he questioned me about my education, putting pressure on me to describe classes I had no idea about. I just wanted to get in the car and drive away, mainly because I knew I was already a couple days late to register and get situated with my new roommate (the "yacht" kid in Boston). I had barely recovered from the long, 48-hours-with-no-sleep drive that had just ended the night before—3000 miles or so in total. So I was horribly impatient, and ultimately pretty horrible to him, my dying father.

Finally, after parrying his several questions I'd had all I could take. Words flew out of my mouth that I've wished ever since I could have taken back.

"You never loved me," I said, angrily. And saw my mother cringe right afterwards. I pretty much just walked out the porch door, got in my car and drove away. It was a blur, heading down Highway 101, through LA, Barstow, Yuma, arriving at college in Tucson, Arizona, a quick 11 hours later.

CHAPTER FIVE
Love/Dropout/Cook

Time to tell the tale of some more real-life ramifications, what occurred after I magically landed the Hyannis dishwashing job when my Boston friend couldn't get one for himself. When we met back at University of Arizona at the beginning of the Fall term—he had recruited me as his roommate—his anger boiled over, as you'll soon see, which ultimately supplied me with a wife and two adopted kids.

*   *   *

Within the scope of actually declining the grill job and returning to college, I didn't know that my fate was soon to be altered by my friend Mark, who had come to resent my success. When I had visited him back in Boston during my dishwashing gig, I'd heard his mother berate him;

"Rick got a job and he doesn't even live here!

Rick could, but not you?"

I imagine that she probably kept on his case for the rest of the summer, repeating that litany over and over, "Rick could, but not you! Through no fault of my own, I had become a hated object in his life.

REAL STORY—Tucson/Six-Pack, 1964

Arriving in Tucson, early September, 1964, I met Mark in an apartment that he had rented for us as "roommates" (with a third roommate also aboard). Yes, I'd returned to college, because of turning down the grill job.

Later that day, after rendezvousing with my friend Tim, and us swinging back to my new apartment in his jeep, I grabbed a six-pack of beer out the frig (figuring I'd just replace it later) and shared it with my friend. Ironically, I didn't drink beer at that time, so I was just being a nice guy to supply the booze.

Tim was a chemical engineering major and local Tucson kid—he figured that he'd work in the mining industry after graduation, just like his dad had done.

We drove around a while, then stopped by at his

mother's house where he was living—I watched him drink another couple of the beers while I didn't partake, not being a beer-lover—and we headed back to my apartment after dark. No one was back yet so I just went to bed in the room I'd been assigned earlier. I was pretty wiped out from doing the one-day drive from California, so went out like a light.

Suddenly I was awakened by loud talking—someone using strong language. I drowsily opened my eyes and looked toward the door, now cracked open and letting bright light in. It was Mark, talking in a really mad voice.

"I want you out of here tomorrow," he almost shouted. "You stole our roommates beer and he's real pissed off. So we don't want you here!" And he slammed the door, for which I was grateful because my face was by then full of tears; my feelings were hurt and I knew I shouldn't have forgotten to replace that six-pack.

I conked right out again, waking up the next morning feeling sad, also nervous that I now had to find some new place to live. I tried to think straight while I got dressed and stuffed clothes back in my bag.

I'd have to see if there was a student rental bulletin board or something. I was already three days late for classes, so wasn't exactly off to a good start.

All dressed and emerging from my room, I was relieved that Mark wasn't around. Certainly didn't want to deal with him again—I would get food someplace else—and started off walking toward school after stowing my clothes in the Plymouth's trunk. As I recall, I didn't meet anyone else on the sidewalk (everyone in that neighborhood was probably a student and already at their 7:30AM classes).

A block from the University of Arizona campus, about a half-block up from the stoplight, I spotted a sign stuck in the front lawn of my future-to-be wife's bungalow-style house. The words, "FOR RENT, COTTAGE IN BACK, $50" seemed like the answer to my prayers. I didn't have the leeway to care what it looked like, or how big or small it was. I'd just take it sight unseen, to get settled enough to attend classes.

I climbed the eight or ten steps up to the front door, knocked and heard nothing. Peering into the hazy, poorly-lit front parlor through a lace curtain I saw no one, but refused to leave until my housing problem was solved. Finally I spied a slowly moving figure emerging from the darkness. The door opened to reveal an old woman, white-haired, around five feet tall.

"Yes?" she asked, as if I was a salesman or something unrelated to the sign out front. "Can I help you?" I quickly blurted out, "I want to rent your cottage," and after a pause she livened up, saying, "Oh...OK. Come in then."

With that, I followed my soon-to-be great grandmother-in-law to a table where a hand-written rental agreement was waiting.

Now, what were the ramifications of taking that rental, that particular one that had stopped me in my tracks on that fresh September morning? Mainly I wouldn't have met my future wife (call her Donna), and wouldn't have met her two young daughters from her first marriage, whom I later adopted.

I do realize that most everyone's life has moments like this, ironic and meaningful instances where their life goes off in a new direction, so I hope I'm not being too over-dramatic here. But isn't it kind

of mind-blowing how a small misstep (borrowed beer!)
can impact your entire life.

Just as I could have easily ended up living in
Hyannis, maybe marrying Rita, doing chef's work until
I got a 1-A designation from the draft board, the REAL
REALITY of my decision to marry Donna and take on
the raising of her two kids did a radical shift, maybe
saving me from the military draft. My later adoption of
her two girls finalized in an Oakland, California court,
removed the threat of a Vietnam draft for good. Also,
getting married helped get my life back on track for art-
making. Me, the kid who, at age 7, spent three
consecutive days painting a realistic-as-I-could image
in watercolor of our small house, when we lived a
while in Sarasota, Florida, for my father's health.

CHAPTER SIX
Video & Film/Babysitter

My next life-altering decision I made (we're up to the year 1970 now) was <u>not</u> dismissing an offer to take a video class, offered right in the middle of my sculpting days at college. I came so close to giving the seat away...as you'll read, which would have meant never making a video/film, or never writing a book about how to produce a feature film "at used-car prices."

REAL-STORY—Casting Bronze/Don Rich, 1970
OK, so there I was, happily watching a teacher (later friend) Don Rich, weld my white bronze castings together. The artwork consisted of a pair of "eagle' wings about 20" high, that I had designed to tie together in a knot at the top points (like a shoelace), held up by a white bronze base. Don was an expert at working metals and I was very thankful that he agreed to do the difficult arc welding it took, to join these two pieces together. And since he was helping me at a

level way beyond "teacher aiding student," I decided to surprise him with some pay. Since I had recently acquired a very special sterling silver railroad watch, with an etching of a steam locomotive on the back side, I decided to honor his effort by giving him a choice. Either $40 (I showed him the bills in my hand) or...(and here's where I removed the watch from my pocket)...THIS. His eyes lit up, and of course he wanted the watch!

I was glad that I hadn't dishonored our interaction without gifting him. And the welds held, giving my largest cast sculpture to date a way to present it on a high stand. But back to how "video" figured into that day.

In the midst of me standing with Don, while he illuminated the walls of the sculpture studio with bright arc welding, up came a fellow student to talk to me about something.

"Hi. You're Rick, right?"

"Yep," I said, wondering what he wanted.

"I learned that you are in a video class, Phil's class, and wonder if I could get that seat if you decide not to do it.

Phil Makanna, now known for his photography and books, "Ghosts," about vintage airplanes from WWII and earlier, had asked me to join his class weeks earlier, because he liked my sculptures. Thinking then, about being in a video studio—moviemaking with bright white, and glaring lights, intrusive, probably with a person on-camera recording one's every freckle—seemed like the last place I thought I'd ever want to be. So as a camera-shy person I weakened, and told the guy, "Sure, OK, you can have it." He seemed overjoyed, and quickly turned, heading at a fast clip toward the registration office in the distance. He got about 15 feet in that direction before I had a change of heart.

"Actually," I called out, "I've changed my mind. I'm going to keep the class."

I don't remember his sad or disappointed face as I shut him down, but I do know that thinking about it while he was walking quickly away, I suddenly couldn't accept it. I realized that the challenges of such a new thing—moviemaking—could be a correct idea to pursue. And that there was a sort of tingling in my skin—feeling that I had just enough confidence to jump into such an unknown activity. So, in the few seconds I had to think about it before the student took my place (bye, bye making movies), I'd examined my aversion to change, and threw caution—and fear—to the wind. *YES*, I said, maybe to the universe, *I'm ready to bust out of what I think of myself, to be a little bit new.*

Without the latest praise I'd received from my metal castings, and receiving full scholarships there at school, I probably would have let it go. Believe me, my decision-making, to take that class or not, was of the subtlest nature. Thinking about my career in movies and books—my efforts have surpassed 50 years—I have to put this off-the-cuff decision into the category of MOST important, and definitely, a turning point in my life.

As it was, since I did dive into video, later film, I submitted a plea to the Head of Graduate Studies, Dr. Schmidt, to have a dual Master's degree, in "Sculpture and Film." And he had graciously said, I'll see what I can do. Happily. after submitting a video (transferred from 16MM) entitled, *The Legal Operation*, as my graduate project, that request was granted.

BUT, what if I hadn't taken Phil's video class?

What if I had just stuck to the metal sculpting, casting artworks, and not tried live-action media? I would have graduated in Sculpture only, and, if fortunate, probably then taught that discipline. Hopefully, I would have snagged a job at one of the very few college level gigs available there in the Bay Area (still getting to be around my little kids). Here's my ALTERNATE fantasy, if I'd never taken that leap into the unknown.

*   *   *

ALTERNATE UNIVERSE #6

Teaching art classes wasn't much of a stretch since I had, after all, been attending such things for over four years before I graduated. But some of the students in my "studio class" seemed like a completely new breed. Not quite troublemakers, but annoying never-the-less. I'd seen a negative trend develop in the last years of my TA time with teacher/friend C.G. Simonds, where no matter what good, accurate criticism he gave to students, they would dismiss his words, often with a snide look or just a turn and rude walk away. The high-point of this kind of critique-proof batch of early-1970s art students was when Charlie was making it clear to a young sculptor that his work was insufficient on several levels, from originality, to form, content and overall quality.

Charlie may of over-stepped a bit when he said, *Not even a good sculpture for your bathroom,* but all he'd really done is match the kid's over-blown ego. Anyway, the kid seemed unfazed. A somewhat over-confident and bold individual, the student listened impatiently then dropped the bomb, saying, "Well it doesn't really matter what you think, because it's been sold for $700." And actually, that worked pretty well for shutting Charlie down, and making it hard to have a comeback in front of the nine students other students present (including me) at this bi-monthly critique.

Having done as much as a teacher could do, Charlie moved on to someone else. *They aren't paying me enough,* I heard him grouse later, *to babysit a bunch of spoiled rich kids taking art classes.*

Well, by the time I was caught in the art teaching game, it had gotten decidedly worse. I was getting around $6,000 a year (forget ever getting out of an apartment into a real house, even though that amount in 2023 dollars would be $45,201! But we're talking 1971, and rents in the San Francisco/Bay Area where I probably would have been teaching—probably in the same sculpture studio of my alma mater; California College of Arts and Crafts—would have left nothing for savings. Not bad, but still not enough to get a dwelling in California and still eat and clothes oneself.

As in REAL LIFE, I would have probably gone a while without a girlfriend, still taking care of my little kids from a first marriage, whom I picked up on Fridays and returned them to school on Monday mornings. In many ways, their company made my shabby two-room apartment seem almost liveable. And as I amassed artworks the children created over the weekends I exhibited them gladly, pinning them to the strip of wall above the wainscoting that ran room to room. Three 8 1/2" X 11" sheets of decorated paper. one under the other, filled the spaces nicely.

On Mondays it was back to teaching art, and believe me, what was becoming considered "art" was rapidly changing. No longer are we talking about the kind of cast metal sculptures I'd made. More conceptual stuff was constantly sneaking in, and I had to roll with the punches. Here are some examples:

One girl had come to class with all her dirty underwear stuffed into a glass vase—jammed in, really—with some kind of red dye poured over and around the cloth items. She'd capped it all at the top by pouring in melted wax, letting that cool, then scratching in the title "Blood Girl" in the hardened wax surface. Remember, my job, as a sculpture teacher was to give feedback and help the students that came through the studio to solve production problems. I was supposed to facilitate the successful production of 3-D objects that "spoke" to people—that's what art was supposed to do in my book. And actually her visual "cacophony" did do that, on some level. Here's a glimpse of how the critique went, for her bloody undies artwork, while the small class of about ten students looked on.

"OK, Sky," I began, "What exactly do we have here?"

"Well, it's my master-bate..ing–I mean master-piece."

Good chuckle emits from most of the student present. The females in the room nod in some sort of agreement, that YES, that's a topic that they can wrap their mind around. In any case, it's me who's on the spot, in the headlights so to speak. So I continue—it's how I get paid! I'd like to still have an apartment, still put food on the table. If I <u>can't</u> survive this critique, without the registrar or president of CCAC getting a complaining note that I'm (a) a feminist-basher, (b) a chauvinist pig, (c) a racist (did I mention the girl is African American?), and (d) just a stupid teacher, who doesn't even understand a master-BATING-masterwork, I'll be one lucky mother-fucker..

"OK," I began again, "Let's take a look at the effect your work has had on our little group." Some of the people there gave a little smile—maybe the men, thinking how deep the shit will be as I continue, while the women were inwardly tickled at me being forced to take the work from Kesha seriously.

"It is possible that this approach to a sculpture—that tells a story—is a type of breakthrough in the realm of narrative art." (That was my lifeline...)

"And so, dear class, I want to hear what you have to say about this piece breaking the wall of old art, to say something completely new...about life, real-life, and all things connected to 1970s women in general.

"And while I'll be very interested in hearing from our female counterparts (I glance around me), I want to hear from you studs too (laughter all around). I mean *male counterparts.* This artwork needs to find its place in a cruel and often heartless art-world where even the best work, if brand new, is misunderstood, often for decades, until a major critic or gallery owner anoints it."

Kesha is just staring, watching me talk. And from what I can determine by her facial expression, which is pretty neutral, part of her must know I'm handling it, handling her being on the spot with me. We're kind of on the same team. Anyway, this is when I get my next bright idea.

"I want each person here to speak about Kesha's sculpture as if it is the most amazing breakthrough in the history of art, a MASTERPIECE so brilliant and fresh that you, the expert, will gush forth, while backing up your observation with some sort of serious anaylsis. Before you start—John, you'll be first to go—please explain who you are from this list; (1) a writer at The New York Times, (2) a top Gallery owner, or (3) a very important art historian. You must state your credentials, and then let the critique fly."

John didn't begin right away, seemed to need a nudge, so I gave one.

"This exercise is important to your grade for this semester, maybe as much as a fourth of the final grade. And there will be other similar play-acting critiques during the remainder of the semester."

With the words, *Good luck, John,* I backed away from the center of the studio, and used my outstretched arms to do a sort of bow in John's direction, indicating the floor was his and his alone.

Slowly, hesitantly he took center stage there in the middle of the cement floor, standing on the scruffy-looking surface where things heavy and dirty had been dragged to and fro for months. A sculptor's paradise, in a sense, but the decor was unimportant. John started out a little stuttery, then seemed to get the hang of being the center of attention.

"Hello, Kesha. My name is John Hammond, and I'm the Director of the Whitney Museum...in New York City." (He gave me a glance and received an approving nod, since I was happily surprised to see that he could play my game). Kesha, to give her credit, held her own too, giving John's words her undivided attention as he launched in.

"I received word from an associate here in California that I should make a trip west, specifically to visit your studio and see some ground-breaking art for myself. And I'm pleased to say that what you've created here—"Bottled Red"—is everything I hoped it would be. If I may, I must state that your creation must now be considered a masterpiece, in the same league as Marcel Duchamp's "Fountain," Monet's water lilies, and Picasso's "Guernica."

Kesha has developed a wide smile by this point. Almost bubbling up to a clenched laugh. After all, John's role-playing had reached an over-the-top dimension, and I could tell several other classmates were ready to burst forth with laughter. Perhaps they

kept themselves muted down a bit because they knew
that they and their sculptural works would be next, to
be spotlighted and discussed in the following critiques.
So there was a little caution reflected on their faces as
John tried to sum things up.

"You certainly will not remain an
"undiscovered West Coast artist" much longer. I plan
to utilize my leadership at the Whitney Museum to
celebrate your fine work, give it the attention it
deserves. You can tell, I think, how excited I am, in
making this discovery—your major work joining
others, in the canon of American Art of the 20th
Century. With my authority, I can now promise you a
one-woman show at the Whitney Museum."

When John stopped his "excessive-praise"
speech, there was a couple second pause before all the
students applauded, while Kesha maintained a funny
look on her face. She had gotten into the performance
as we all had—John as "art expert"—and it seemed the
kid had a future as an actor as well as sculptor, and I
told him so.

"Damn, John, you have some impressive
chops," is all I seemed to be able to say. Also,

"Well...very well done. You brought the moment for Kesha. Nice job. And—I chuckled—nice use of the word *canon*." Others smirked at this mention.

"Anyone want to respond? Kesha?"

Kesha was now in an introspective mood, and who could blame her. When a person's big artist-ego gets stroked at the highest level, even for pretend, it is a bit overwhelming. And that's what had just happened. John had said everything she ever wanted to hear about her work. Yes, all artists wish they could experience that level of praise from the most important and influential art critics, museum directors, fellow associates. And she had gotten it, full tilt.

Still reeling, Kesha dredged up a response—to her credit. She continued the roll-playing performance that John had initiated.

"Thank you, Mr. Hammond. I'm most pleased that the Whitney has offered me a show. Thank you, and your board of directors. It's a great honor, for which I'll always be grateful."

Now everyone was fully involved, Kesha's acting, on-point, pretty much brought the house down.

It was surprising, even to me, how real the entire experience felt. Each student, men and women, had allowed themselves to believe Kesha's art had broken through, got recognition. It was a WOW moment, and I must admit I enjoyed it, even feeling that I was a pretty fuckin' good director!

If only I had let that other kid take my place, registering for VIDEO, I could have had the calmer, "out-of-the-spotlight" life of a quiet sculptor/teacher. But, NOOOO (nod to John Belushi). My fate-line was in the Media Arts, which required many moments like that odd critique, when I introduced "performance" to my normal teaching activities.

It was obvious I could get people to act, like sculpture student John had done in my manufactured "fantasy" art critique. That directing skill-set had came in handy later, during the next 50 years of moviemaking, using non-actors to act as characters in a story, and tell their most important stories to a camera.

REAL STORY—$50 Cabin/Crashing ('69)

After this little "art school critique" exercise, another real-life experience comes to mind. For the period of time when I was just wandering the streets of Berkeley after my split from Donna—adrift in my own confused thoughts about where I belonged, doing what, living how—I spotted a "House For Rent" sign in front of a two story brown shingle house not far from the U.C campus in Berkeley. "$50" was also advertised on the sign (I'd seen one like that before...). So I decided to climb the stairs and check it out.

At the top landing, which opened right up into a large attic room, sat an elderly couple. They didn't bother to move from their two big cushy chairs, but did acknowledge my appearance. A little bit like a fly to the fly-paper. As it turned out, I was their current play-thing, or at least a person who might help them get other hippies in their rental next door evicted. Within a few moments that's what was discussed, but the initial talk took a while to get to the point.

Man: "Hello, can we help you?"

Me: "Yeah, I guess. Just wondering if the house next door is still for rent?"

The sign stuck in the grass out front had said $50...for a cute brown shingle cabin. Even I could imagine getting the money together to live there. After all, when school got back in session, I did earn $160/month at CCAC art college, as a double-TA in the foundry.

Woman: "Maybe. But there are other...people...who haven't paid their rent...in there now."

Me: "Oh. Then will it come up for rent later...or..."

Woman (cutting me off): "No, it's for rent now. As soon as we get the people out."

Me (repeating myself): "Oh."

Woman (allowing for a little pregnant pause): "In fact. If you could go over there and throw those hippie deadbeats out... we'll give you the first month's rent for free."

Me (my third repeated exclamation): "Oh."

So with that fairly unusual offer (free rent!) I decided to at least go over there, knock on their door, and see what fellow hippie deadbeats looked like. I may have added an OK, before I headed back down the stairs. But believe me, I never had it in my mind to throw anyone out, never would have. I put the exercise in the mental space of just something to do for a few minutes that warm Berkeley early July morning, in my state of; trying-to-be-mindless-and not think-of-my-failed-marriage.

Knock, knock. And a voice called softly through the partially open front door, *"Come in."* I cleared the door open and saw just a young woman, long hippie-type dress on, standing at a table about eight feet away, stirring whatever was in the pot on the stove. As I entered the space I must have gotten one hell of a "contact high," because I just remember approaching her in a sort of slow motion floating sensation, and gently kissing her on the lips. Now, there was absolutely no sexual feeling involved in that kiss, no actual attraction to her as a female human. I don't remember her being in any way "attractive," just a young female cooking something, in the cool interior of a low-light studio-room where the kitchen was not separated from any other part of the space. It was as if the universe was dictating my actions, as if I really hadn't made any kind of decision in the matter. It was simply what was happening, without any idea in my head.

It still surprises me that I would have felt such an easy permission to be that personal with someone I had only set eyes on three or four seconds before. And she hadn't thought anything special about it either, just asked if I was hungry. And when I nodded she spooned some soup into a bowl.

To me, trying to explain this unusual mini-event in the midst of my marriage break-up summer of 1969, pretty well captures what the hippie thing was all about. If the idea of a one-world family was in the air, it came that close to being true.

Throwing her out of her rented house was never mentioned, and why would it have been? I had just wondered who lived there, and enjoyed finding someone who I could easily relate to—a fellow member of the hippie sub-culture.

*   *   *

NOW...here comes the next ALTERNATE Universe projection. What if she had asked me, *Do you want to live here...for awhile? With me? And Junior?* In those days—not really living anywhere, just being another street-person who could survive by sleeping outside (in summer months), I would likely have considering answering, *OK*. It might have dawned on me that maybe having some known place to sleep would be a good thing.

Eating my $.25 sandwiches from Old Joe's grocery store off Telegraph Avenue at 51st Street in Oakland (see "Old Joe's Sandwiches" in my Memoir, <u>12 DEAD FROGS and Other Stories</u>), and wandering the streets, often at night, would have ultimately gotten me some grief.

In fact, just a few days after this odd occurrence of checking out the $50 cottage and the "neutral" kiss on the lips (but not moving in), I called up my teacher friend, Charlie, and asked if he had a place where I could crash. He said, *Yes,* and told me to meet him at his girlfriend's place on McGee St, Berkeley—a huge Victorian house with a turret on top. And she generously gave me the expansive, empty attic space in which to crash (a waiting mattress helped). And that ended my short-lived homeless summer experience.

ALTERNATE UNIVERSE #7a

Let's say I moved into the $50 cabin, which took no effort because I had no suitcase, no stuff, just what I was wearing. Hippie Woman didn't talk much at first, and neither did I, so there were the two of us, me suddenly living in the rental house with "the deadbeats." I wondered how many more of us hippies would end up in there, if the elderly couple kept sending wanderers like me over to kick hippies out.

That first night with Jane was pretty nice. Her child was a sweet little girl named Sky, with blond hair in baby-curls—what not to love? And although I slept with Jane in her queen-sized bed (that's all there was) it didn't seem too crowded. At some point she did turn over in my direction. said "Goodnight," and did land a soft kiss. Again, there was no urging of anything sexual, but I imagined that could change. Not wise, though, since the father of Sky was around, and I figured he wouldn't be too happy to be supplanted by some hippie guy making out with his wife (or at least girlfriend, if they were unmarried).

Woke up more rested than usual, and could smell coffee and food happening feet away, with some baby talk in the air. With some shafts of light emitting from the open window, the scene looked a little like a painting I'd seen somewhere—Mother and Child—maybe an English 19th century artwork of some sort. If this was all a dream it was a pretty pleasant one, that is until Junior Sr. showed up.

He was a big guy, maybe 240 pounds, and anyone that much bigger (I was just 180) can be intimidating. When I felt that sensation of fearing someone who was heavier and towered over me (Sr. was probably 6'4"), I immediately worked to difuse it. I certainly didn't enjoy being manipulated by that age-old, back to Neanderthal Man survivalist fight-or-flight response, when it was <u>you</u> against <u>them</u> on the most primal level.

Another hill to climb was that I could tell he suspected me of being a possible love interest to Jane. He did check me out—I caught a few of his glances—that seemed to broadcast that jealousy, and I worked fast to dispel that too. I introduced myself, and hoped he'd get more secure in understanding that the scene was still his and his alone.

"Hi. Jane said you'd drop in today. I'm Rick, and I just..."

"Yeah, yeah, she told me she had a roommate. You gonna help with rent, right?"

I hoped that my reaction, my "gulp," hadn't been too noticeable. I hadn't had time to think about rent and stuff like that. I realized all I could say was what was expected.

"Sure. Yeah."

"Half would be $25," Junior Sr. said, with a look of seriousness. "Isn't that right?" he added.

If I paid that amount then his responsibility to keep a roof over his kid head would be much less, so I'd be on firmer and safer ground. And anyway, how could I say no to that big, threatening guy? And because of the color of his skin—he was a black man—that probably added to the intimidation.

"Yuh gonna do that? Right?"

"Yeah," I repeated again.

"You will," he stayed on it, and I was wondering if we'd ever get off the topic. So I again spelled it out, with a full sentence of commitment to making a payment.

"Yes, I can cover the $25...Each month...as long as I stay here."

Junior nodded, finally approving of my answer enough to look away and call out his kids name.

"SKY!" was called, loud enough that he woke up his daughter from her nap in the other room. Waaa, waa. Jane went in, scooped up blondie, and returned, easing the half-awake kid into her father's big, broad arms. Daddie broke into a grin, looked over at the mother of his kid and seemed transformed into a happy camper. I tried to disappear myself, walking to the other end of the cabin, to the frig, and removed a half-empty bottle of orange juice I had bought around the corner the day before.

After Junior Sr. split and things settled back down again— Sky back in crib, Jane on the bed sewing something, me at the dinner table reading a year-old Time magazine—the thoughts of "Am I a racist" popped into my thoughts. How programmed was I, reacting the way I did to a masculine Black man in my near proximately. I let my mind wander back to my early years, growing up in Chicago, when I'd had a few interactions with gangs, both White and Black. And actually, the White gangs that accosted me outnumbered black ones two-to-one.

REAL STORY—Escaping Racism

One time a group of White kids had formed a circle around me when I entered the alley behind my house on the South Side, and took turns punching me, while a bunch of taller, older boys formed a larger circle around them. I did notice that the punches (to my middle section, not face) lacked the ability to really hurt me. I was scared, of course, but surprisingly not paniced in any way. The whole thing was so curious—I was around 12. But as the beating dragged on I figured that I should at least try to cry, and sort of faked it enough for the older guys' satisfaction, and they suddenly calling it off.

One of the bigger outside guys approached me and handed me a brand new roll of Lifesavers candies, telling me to not tell anyone about what happened. It was then that I defined what had transpired as simply a "learning exercise," older brothers teaching their younger siblings how to fight.

An earlier interaction I had with the White baddies in Chicago was when an older kid approached me on 47th Street, that separated 50-plus blocks of Blacks from the Whites). I was getting ready to slip on my new roller skates near the IC (Illinois Central Railroad) train station overpass. He was intimidating enough that when he asked if he could just try them on I blurted out, "You're just going to steal them." He answered, unconvincingly, *No. I'm not.* After I reluctantly handed them over, he put them on and skated away.

Strangely, the next time I ran into him he was chasing me across IC train tracks, where if you stepped on the third rail (or fell!) you'd be electrocuted. Luckily, neither of us misstepped. When I got to a train platform I was able to shinny up onto it, and when the bully arrived just after me, he couldn't.

He ended up pleading with me, close to tears, to help him when he saw a train coming, That mean, tough guy, was transformed into a half-sobbing, scared, little kid. That was an eye-opener for me, as I pulled him up, out of danger.

My next gang experience, with Black kids, was the most frightening as you'll see. My buddy Mack and I decided to ride our bikes from 47th St. down to the Loop (Chicago's center for business, movie theaters, big stores, museums, etc.), about seven miles away. And at around a third of the distance, as we rolled through a large wooded park, we were suddenly attacked by a large group of somewhat small, young Black boys, emerging from behind what seemed like every tree on both sides of our path. It was actually a well-orchestrated ambush by possibly 20 kids, all motivated to capture us, steal from us (our bikes, money) and possibly do us harm if we didn't gladly part with our things.

The young leader, a guy taller than the rest, ordered Mack to give him his bike. Mack refused and the kid hit him right in the eye, making my friend tumble backwards over his two-wheeler.

Then, the leader turned his attention to me. "Give me your money!" he demanded. I reached into my pockets which were jammed with all the quarters, dimes, pennies I had brought along for spending. I wrapped my fingers around all the change until I couldn't hold anymore, removed hands from pockets and threw the coins as far away as I could, in a wide arc. Instantly the entire gang scattered, each member running frantically toward the coins, diving to the ground, trying to scoop up change, filling their pockets.

While this was happening I was trying to roust Mack, get him back on his bike for our escape. But before I could fully accomplish that I heard a booming voice coming loudly from somewhere behind me.

"Hey you kids. Stop bothering those white boys. Leave them alone!"

I looked over, and there was a well-dressed Black teenager— our savior—making sure that ruckus was ended and that we could safely clear out, retreat, bike our way back to our side of the city.

So when I wonder to what degree I'm racist or not, I recall and embrace that time when the White Chicago gangs were nowhere near as honorable or as gracious as the young Black man who stepped in that day in 1955, on the Lakeshore, and put a halt to Black-on-White violence.

*   *   *

ALTERNATE UNIVERSE #7b—(Sr.'s Criminals)

As I've said before, whenever Senior came by the small cabin where I was temporarily living (in my mind at least), he was suspicious that I might, in some way, be infringing on his scene. Most of us humans can pick up the kind of vibes Sr. was emitting, and I was no exception. And without dulling my senses with beer or marijuana, which I noticed Jane used fairly often, I felt a little off-balance. I vacillated between wanting to confront him, or just letting it slide. After all, within three weeks a new semester at my art college in Oakland was set to begin, where I'd again be focused on casting hot metal to make art, all the while earning good TA money helping other students do the same. So what was happening there in Berkeley, was kind of moot. Yes, I felt friendly to Jane, and yes, I was vulnerable just by proximately, to possibly getting more deeply involved. I wondered what would happen in the next few weeks.

As days went on—I'd take a toke here, a beer there, me even helping to change a few diapers for

Sky—I realized that at some point I would disappear down a rabbit hole, called "new relationship," maybe even "new baby/kid," even before the diapers were dry from what I'd call my *real* marriage. Couldn't see myself drifting from one mess to another.

In the middle of these various thoughts on the matter of living, while lazing around with Jane and little Blondie, Sr. came by and seemed to be suddenly making an effort to get to know me better. It started out with him saying, "Hey, Rick, let's grab a beer." This offer did surprise me, because up to that point I don't think he had said two words to me, like I'd been invisible and now was suddenly 3-D. I was a little too naive back then, to see the possibility that it could be some kind of trap.

We stopped at LaVal's restaurant in upper Berkeley, right above the UC campus where a narrow pizza parlor/narrow movie theatre gave students access to snacks and alcohol. We sat at the inside picnic tables drinking from a pitcher of beer while eating some slices. Still not much talking was going on, even after I gave Sr, the indirect compliment of saying his child was showing new development skills. Between a few bites of my pepperoni topping I also added something like, *Your kid's getting pretty big...walking soon.*

Sr. barely looked up from the Berkeley Barb he was perusing. I took two more bites, took another swallow from my beer, and opened my Barb. His response never came regarding his daughter, but I was surprised by what I heard. next He invited me to accompany him to some friend's house in the Oakland Hills. It was odd to find myself sitting next to that imposing Black man, father of Sky, lover of Jane. Strange that I'd even come in contact with a guy like that. But somehow my life's path had delivered me to that moment. As we drove toward Oakland I have to admit I was a bit apprehensive.

His Studebaker was an old one—looked like a WWII dive-bomber in front—but it made it up the road into Montclair, a ritzier part of the Oakland highlands, and he pulled it into a driveway. With a knock on the front door that sounded like a code, the kind gangsters used in black-and-white movies—bap, bap, bonk, bap, bonk–the door cracked open. Another Black guy acknowledged him with just, *Hey*, and I followed both of them in. In the next room there were maybe ten or twelve Black guys, a couple of Whites also, seated around a large circular table low to the ground. So all were seated on the floor on cushions. It was hard to miss the fact that various piles of drugs were in front of each person, plus some guns—revolvers–next to some of them. I tried not to reveal that I was taken aback, call it *scared*. Sr. sat in, with me settling back into a cushion against a wall. He removed some rolled up bills and one of the inhabitants slid a plastic bag his way. I was uncomfortable and hoped we'd be back outside soon, but Sr. had other plans.

"This is Rick—he's a artist," said Sr. and maybe a third of the stoned customers/dealers looked up. Someone said, "Oh yeah?" Sr. kept going.

"He makes shit out of metal..." adding "melted metal."

Another guy looked up, "Like swords, Samurai?"

Now Sr. left me to answer, by turning his gaze to me, putting me on the spot. What was I to say?

"Um...not exactly. Just weird art stuff. But I guess someone could make a sword-like thing that way."

Another guy—curly hair as I recall, wearing a heavy leather vest with a '38 revolver right where he sat—blurted out, "How much?"

I was confused and didn't answer right away, so he added, "For a Samurai sword?"

I could tell that Sr. was starting to get a kick out of this, and that certainly didn't relieve the pressure I was feeling. Part of my brain was running in circles, trying to figure out (1) the "correct" answer, and (2) how not to offend the scary guy who asked.

When the guy—I'll call him "Vest"—looked up at me with his mean-looking, ex-convict eyes, I realized I was getting into deeper trouble, and a glance toward Sr. reinforced that, because his vibe said, *See what happens when you fuck with another person's (ex)-wife/mother of your kid?* Fortunately, I hadn't actually fucked anyone, but if I had I would have been shaking in my boots about then. In any case, as another of the undesirable guys also looked up—criminals they were, I now realized—I seriously hoped that I could figure out a quick answer that would unhook me from this bad experience. Here's what I blurted out.

"Never made a sword, but if I ever do I'll give it to Sr.—to drop off here."

Vest seemed satisfied and, with the word, *Cool*, went back to sorting his seeds or whatever he was slowly doing.

Sr. enjoyed the extra bit of prestige—connecting himself to "a sword-maker"—and soon after that we were coasting our way back down to the Berkeley flats and to my drop-off point at the little cottage. I realized then that my new scene was beginning to have too high a psychic cost, for the roof it supplied.

The next morning, just like any other (it was by now mid-July) I got dressed, put two $20s on the kitchen table (Jane was still asleep in the bedroom with Sky), and split. I'm not sure that the term "split" translates for foreign students from other countries, but most people know that it means *LEAVE* in hippie slang—and that's what I did.

And I didn't look back.

Was that cruel?

Or at least ungallant or impolite?

Hope not too much. But in that summer of '69 people did come and go, and that's simply what I did.

Back on the street again, I returned to the old preoccupation with wondering where I would spend the night, especially worrisome when darkness enveloped me around 8:45PM that time of year. My solution to beat the expected dread (including fear of future interaction with Sr. as part of 'cabin life') was to just keep hitching.

Sometimes 11:30PM to midnight, even later; 1:00-4:00AM, I'd be stationed there on University Avenue, Berkeley, standing next to the road with my thumb out. At least I *appeared* functional, doing something, not being weird or suspect (as in, *police pulling a person in for questioning for vagrancy*). Was I "beating the system?" Donno. But I did make it through a few nights not sleeping much, before sculptor teacher/friend Charlie drove by, noticed me and offered his girlfriend's Berkeley Victorian as my crash pad.

OK! Of course, my living in the cabin—crashing with Jane and Sky, and Senior coming around—didn't ever happen beyond the odd friendly kiss and a bowl of soup offered by the young woman when I checked out the $50 rental. And I never tried to cast a Samurai sword at the CCA(C) art school foundry, although I would have loved to see the looks from fellow students and Charlie, for trying that!

Fantasizing about this Cabin Story & Sr.'s Criminal Friends made another REAL memory flash across by mind, an odd trip that I experienced in 1969, at the beginning of the REAL homeless summer, also involving a trip into the Oakland Hills.

REAL STORY—Going Nowhere

The last time I'd been up there, actually above the cloud cover on a misty evening, was when I'd been hitchhiking on Telegraph Avenue after being bored and wanting to leave that scene during my short-lived homeless days. When an old Chevy half-ton with three kids my age in the front seat pulled over, I jumped in the back. And after it got rolling the driver stuck his head out the window and asked, *Where yuh going?* My answer (which well-expressed my entire outlook on life as a wandering, rootless, confused, semi-homeless divorced guy), was—*Nowhere.* The long-haired, mid-twenties hippie driver—a version of myself, then called back in appropriate hippie-slang, *Groovy,* and without missing a beat he accelerated the old pickup, heading it toward wherever the hell he and his friends were going, allowing me to be their unmotivated passenger.

The pickup rattled its way past the Oakland highlands, and I remember how soothing the damp air felt on my face as we encountered a fairly thick band of fog before traveling above it. We arrived at the driveway of an older house and I just sat there in the pickup bed as the riders removed an old sewing machine from near where I was sitting and carried it away. So I was alone for maybe five or seven minutes. A funny feeling, I remember, sitting there, peering at trees, houses, phone lines, with no sign of life anywhere.

As soon as they returned we rolled our way back downhill, arriving back within minutes to the Ave., exactly where I'd been picked up. I jumped out when the driver stopped, who then called back, *OK?* I thanked him––a nice round-trip diversion from reality—and walked on, heading into the busy foot traffic of newly-minted University of California students; studying, eating, hobnobbing, experiencing the beginning of their adulthood a block away from the Berkeley campus.

*   *   *

WRAP-UP

So, where are we at now? I've criss-crossed my Fantasy/What-Ifs stories with real life experiences quite a few times, and maybe it's time to release you readers back to your own Fantasy/REAL lives. I hope this back-and-forth has helped some people make decisions differently (if they need to...), so that real-life is as fruitful and dynamic as it's supposed to be, without too many dangerous bends in the road.

Some wise women say this; "There are no mistakes." *Life is life*, and everything is placed in front of us for the good of our soul's growth and enlightenment. And I've come to believe this.

As I was writing my memoir, <u>TWELVE DEAD FROGS</u>, I finally learned the lesson my own stories were trying to teach. Here it is.

When you carefully examine every so-called "negative moment" in your life, and then open yourself up to realizing the importance of those seemingly random events, how they granted you the hard-won knowledge needed later to survive difficult challenges, the idea of "good" verses "bad" evaporates away. You may be amazed to discover that there are really *no unnecessary experiences*. Let me know by email (<rickschmidtbooks@gmail.com>) if you agree!

*   *   *
*   *
*

The LIFE MAGAZINE that greeted me right after I returned from the hitchhike trip that had taken me to that exact commune in Oregon, early July, 1969.

A rigorous home-grown diet, mystical jargon and meditation in a tepee

In the lodge, above, Nancy reads to herself from the Bible. The children of the commune (below) are expected to help in occasional chores in the garden and kitchen, but spend much of their time in the surrounding woods hunting for berries or playing make-believe.

Above, Sandoz and Twig serve themselves a midday meal of rice, vegetables and fruit. Most of the members do not eat meat. At right, as the coolness of the night comes to the mountains, Ama sits in silent meditation in the tepee he built last summer. He is building a log cabin nearby where he plans to spend the winter with his wife Evening Star and their expected child.

A magazine page shows the same selection of garden-fresh vegetables from which I ate (upper right). Which ingredient made me pass out for an hour after devouring the meal?

diet, mystical jargon and
meditation in a tepee

Above, Sandoz and Twig serve themselves a midday
meal of rice, vegetables and fruit. Most of the members do not eat meat. At right, as the coolness of the
night comes to the mountains, Ama sits in silent meditation in the tepee he built last summer. He is building
a log cabin nearby where he plans to spend the winter
with his wife Evening Star and their expected child.

A close-up of the Oregon Commune food I ate, leading
to my Rip Van Winkle experience.